Orga

Pack

Move!

Strategies and Money-Saving Ideas to Simplify Your Move

Nancy Giehl
Joan Hobbs

SIMPLE MOVES

About the Authors

Organize Pack Move! authors, Joan Hobbs and Nancy Giehl, believe moving is a great time to organize and declutter a household. This brings three rewards—you save money on moving costs by not moving things you don't need, unpacking is much less of a chore because everything is organized and you will quickly relax and enjoy your new home.

Organizational experts Joan and Nancy are owners of Simple Moves; an organizing company that specializes in helping people downsize and move. They have helped hundreds of people organize their belongings before a move and settle into their new homes in the Boulder, Colorado area.

Boulder, Colorado 80303
©2009 by Simple Moves
All rights reserved. Published 2009.

ISBN: 978-0-9825718-0-4 (paper)

Contents

Sorting and Organizing, cont.

Trash and Recycling

Donating and Selling

Donating

Sell It Yourself

Have Someone Sell It for You

PACKING AND MOVING

Planning for Your New Home

Helpful Tips for Every Move

Special Circumstances

CHECKLISTS AND WORKSHEETS
Checklists

Worksheets

How to Use This Workbook

WE'VE HELPED HUNDREDS OF PEOPLE MOVE and we've talked to hundreds more about their moves. Over and over we see people with the same frustrations. They end up spending more money than they need to, waste time because it is hard to prioritize the tasks they need to accomplish and end up physically and emotionally drained. We created this workbook to combat those frustrations.

You're busy, you're moving, you don't have time to read a whole book or spend hours online searching for the information you need. We condensed everything we have learned through experience into a one-page-per-topic workbook, with helpful checklists and worksheets to keep you on track and organized. This concise information is designed to save you money, time and energy.

Organize, Pack, Move! is divided into 6 sections:
- ◢ Preparation and Initial Decisions
- ◢ Organizing for Your Move
- ◢ Donating and Selling
- ◢ Packing and Moving
- ◢ Settling In
- ◢ Checklists and Worksheets

Throughout these pages we refer you to other related articles. You can identify them quickly by their distinctive look, see *Planning the Do-It-Yourself Move (p. 59)*

One of our first recommendations to clients is to keep all moving information in one place. Our workbook gives you valuable tips and strategies, and paired with a three-ring binder with inside pockets to store the paperwork you will be accumulating, you have a perfect combination to keep everything together.

Happy moving!

Joan Hobbs & Nancy Giehl, Owners
Simple Moves
www.simplemoves.net
info@simplemoves.net

Preparation and Initial Decisions

Keep Everything Together

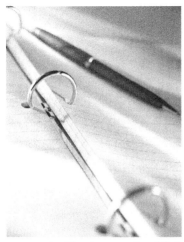

THERE IS A LOT OF PAPERWORK that accumulates when you move. In the confusion, it's easy to lose track of the things you need the most. We've watched many a client scramble through piles of paper searching for a business card or an important document related to their move.

One of the key principles of organizing is to have a place for everything. To help you keep your move organized and everything in one place, designate a space in your home that is your "moving center". It should include:

◢ **This Workbook -** with its easy one-page-per-topic tip sheets, checklist and worksheets.

◢ **A Binder -** a 1" three-ring binder to store all the paperwork you will be accumulating.

◢ **Master contact list -** a running list of the contact information for all things moving related—realtor, moving company, mortgage broker, etc. If your binder has a sleeve on the cover, this is a great place to keep this list.

◢ **A Phone Book -** you'll want to have one handy.

Types of Papers You'll Want to Keep Together

◢ Realtor information
◢ Moving company information
◢ Contracts
◢ Information on your new home
◢ Floor plans
◢ Warranties
◢ Mortgage information
◢ Loan documents
◢ Service agreements
◢ Repair estimates
◢ Insurance information
◢ Home inventory
◢ Resource information

Don't Lose It!
Keep everything in a handy location. Return it there after each use so you'll always be able to find it.

Is Your Move Tax Deductible?

IF YOUR MOVE IS RELATED TO YOUR JOB you may be able to deduct certain moving expenses on your tax return. Job-related moving expenses are direct deductions from your income. If you meet the requirements you will reduce your tax bill.

Here are some general guidelines regarding tax deductible moves. Consult your tax professional for specific information.

You Must Meet Three Tests

To determine if you meet these tests see IRS Publication 521, Moving Expenses and IRS Form 3903, Moving Expense Worksheet. They can be found on the IRS website at *irs.gov*.

- ◢ **Who Can Deduct Moving Expenses?** Generally moving expenses are deductible if your move is job-related. (See Publication 521.)
- ◢ **A Distance Test.** If your new job is 50 miles or farther from your old home to your new workplace you may meet this test. (See the Distance Test Worksheet on Form 3903.)
- ◢ **A Time Test.** In general you must work full time for at least 39 weeks within the 12 months after you move. There are other requirements to this test and specific rules for seasonal workers and self-employed. (See Publication 521.)

What Costs Are Deductible?

First of all, keep all receipts related to your move. Tuck them into one of the pockets of your binder so you have all your documentation in one place. For detailed information on deductible costs see IRS Publication 521.

Generally You Can Deduct

- ◢ All reasonable expenses related to packing and moving your goods
- ◢ Cost of transportation (but not meals) for moving yourself and your family (one-time per person)

Costs That Are NOT Deductible

- ◢ Costs to fix up your old home for sale
- ◢ House hunting costs
- ◢ Storage costs not directly related to moving
- ◢ Expenses and fees for buying and selling your home (i.e. mortgage fees, points, inspections, etc.)
- ◢ Real estate taxes

Create a Home Inventory

AN INVENTORY LIST is a useful tool to keep track of all your belongings during a move. Additionally, it is a very important document in case of a fire or theft. Creating an inventory list alerts you to high-value items that warrant an appraisal before your move.

There are a number of computer programs to help you create your home inventory. Even a simple spreadsheet is fine. Keep a backup copy of the information in your safe deposit box, at work or with a friend or relative.

This is not just a list of your valuables. It is a list of EVERYTHING you own. From the shoes on your closet floor to your garden implements to your antique armoire, you want to document everything. That way, in the event something goes missing after your move, you will have the documentation you need. We have heard countless tales about that one box that got lost during a move. After your list is complete, run it by your insurance agent to confirm your belongings are adequately protected.

Tips for Making a Home Inventory List

- Go methodically through each room of your home.
- Go around the room and film everything. Don't forget to open drawers and cabinets. For high-value items with serial numbers, take a shot of the label with the serial number. Photographs or videos are time savers and they are useful for documenting the condition of your belongings.
- For personal items like clothing, grouping like items together is adequate. List a general amount, (10 dresses, 10 skirts, 15 pants, etc.) and note the shops you frequent the most. This will give a general idea of the value of your wardrobe.
- Provide written documentation for higher value items as well. Using home inventory software or your own spreadsheet, be sure to include the following—description, model, serial number, purchase date, where you bought it and purchase value. For example, do not write "TV," write "50-inch Sony plasma flat screen, purchased at Best Buy in 2007 for $2000, serial #XXX."
- Gather all corresponding documents—purchase receipts, warranties, owner's manuals, appraisals, etc.
- Put everything together in one place.
- This is a time consuming project. If you're pressed for time, at least take a video camera around the house and garage and do a running verbal commentary about everything.

How to Use Our Worksheets and Checklists

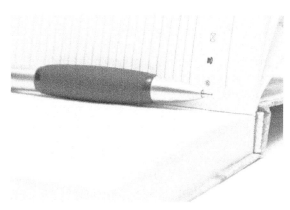

AT THE END OF THIS WORKBOOK, is a section with worksheets and checklists. We developed the lists at the request of our clients. They are comprehensive lists and are there to help you keep track of what you've done and what still needs to be done. Depending on your move, you may not need to accomplish everything on the list. Adapt them to your personal circumstances.

Tasks to Complete
The number of tasks to keep track of and complete for a move can be overwhelming. This checklist is a guide to help you stay on top of everything and keep you from overlooking something essential.

Documents to Keep
You will be sorting through stacks of paper as you prepare for your move. What to keep and what to discard is confusing. This checklist gives you a starting point to help you decide what is necessary to take with you. Note: Many of these papers should travel with you and not be put on a moving van. Read Things to Keep With You (p. 54) for more information.

Notifications to Make
This checklist is divided into nine different categories of people and companies you will need to notify regarding your move, from your vet to the IRS. Personalize this list to with your own service providers. Following this checklist are several notifications worksheets. Take the time to fill out the worksheets so nothing gets overlooked. The notification worksheets are divided into individual sections:

- Address Change Notifications (p. 95)
- Service Cancellations (p. 96)
- New Services (p. 97)
- Service Transfers (p. 98)

Move Yourself or Hire the Pros?

ONE OF THE FIRST DECISIONS TO MAKE when you learn you are moving is what kind of move you want. For young people with few belongings and not much money the do-it-yourself move is the obvious choice. With a corporate relocation or for those who can afford it, a full-service move is the easiest and least stressful option.

For the rest of us, deciding whether or not it is worth paying for packing, loading/unloading and driving a truck is a difficult decision. Add in kids, pets, and a long distance move and the decisions become harder. Below are options to consider in your decision-making.

Different Type of Moves

- **A full do-it-yourself move. You pack, you load, you drive, you unload.** This is a great way to move if you are young and don't have many belongings. If you are a family of four with pets and the accompanying stuff, this will be challenging.
- **You pack and load a truck. A company drives that truck to your new home. You unload and unpack.** This is good for a local move when you have lots of friends and family in the area to help.
- **You pack. A company loads your belongings into their van, drives to your new home and unloads. You unpack.** This works best for time-strapped families on a budget. The heavy lifting is done by someone else but you save money on labor by packing yourself.
- **A full service move. The movers pack, load, drive, unload, and sometimes even unpack for you in your new home.** A plus that usually comes with corporate relocations, this is the way to go if money is no object.

Things to Think About

- Protect yourself. Check with your insurance agent. Make sure, especially if you are hiring day labor to help load or unload, that your homeowner's policy will cover accidents associated with moving.
- If you are doing a price comparison on the types of moves, don't forget to factor in truck fuel, one-way truck rental fees, missed days of work and packing of special items like pianos.
- Your time and energy are important to consider during a move. If finances allow, get as much help as you can.

The Cost of Moving

MOVING IS EXPENSIVE. There are costs common to any move and many people are surprised at the expenses they failed to foresee. Here is a list of potential moving costs.

▲ **Getting your home ready to sell.** Costs include repairs and inspections, painting, house cleaning, carpet cleaning, yard maintenance, window washing, staging and storage.

▲ **Packing/moving services.** Costs vary tremendously from the do-it-yourself move to the full service move. Expenses for services vary depending on what types of items you will be moving and how far you are moving them.

▲ **Packing materials.** If you are a do-it-yourself mover you will have packing material costs. At minimum you'll need boxes, packing tape, packing paper and trash bags. Having the right supplies on hand when you pack will save you time and energy.

▲ **Appraisals/consignment fees.** Sometimes it costs you money to sell things. High value items should be appraised and appraisers typically charge a flat rate or hourly fee.

▲ **Trash removal.** In our experience every move generates significantly more trash than our clients expected. Trash removal services and fees vary greatly across the country and from town to town. Check with your current provider to find out the cost of extra services.

▲ **Insurance.** If you are moving yourself be sure you have moving insurance (or that your current home owners policy protects your belongings). Also, check on personal liability insurance if you have friends or hire workers to do heavy lifting.

▲ **Other services.** These may include pet care, childcare and lawn care.

Recommended Articles

▲ For more detailed information on selling, see the *Selling and Donating* chapter of this workbook

Consider Your Time

MOVING IS INCREDIBLY TIME CONSUMING. In our experience people significantly underestimate the amount of time it takes to accomplish downsizing, decluttering, packing up and moving. It is no wonder moving is considered one of the top three life-stressing events.

We created the table below to give you an idea of the time it takes to accomplish common tasks associated with moving. Depending on how quickly you work and how easily you get sidetracked, any one of these may take significantly longer.

Average Amount of Time to Complete Common House Clearing Tasks

Set up an eBay account—set up account, get PayPal account, learn process, photograph and post item	6 hours
Prep and hold a garage sale	40 hours
Prepare first time listing for Craigslist—learn process, photograph, write ad	2-3 hours
Clean out a crowded two-car garage	12-16 hours
Clean out a storage room	8-12 hours
Sort through office paperwork	8-12 hours

By planning in advance you can save both time and energy. For example, many people decide to donate the things they don't want to keep when they realize how much time it takes to hold a garage sale. Or they decide to hire out certain tasks they originally thought they would take on themselves.

All of the articles in this workbook are designed to help you save your time, your energy or your money. Sometimes one comes at the expense of the other but often you can save on all three.

Hiring a Moving Company

WHEN A MOVING COMPANY comes to give you a bid they will walk through your home to determine what size moving van is needed for the job. Be clear with the company about what you will or will not be taking with you so their bid will be accurate. If something changes, alert the moving company your hired about the changes before moving day to avoid additional, last-minute charges.

Moving Company Advice

- ◢ Get at least three bids. Tell the company giving you an estimate you are receiving other bids.
- ◢ A walk-through of your home by a representative of each company should be required for all bids. Do not accept Internet bids or bids over the phone.
- ◢ Ask the moving company what you can do to save money on your move.
- ◢ Some moving companies charge by the load, others charge an hourly rate based on number of crewmembers—find out.
- ◢ Many movers start charging you from the time they leave their company parking lot. If you live far from the company fleet you will pay more.
- ◢ Find out how many members are on the crew. We've found movers that charge the same rate per hour but the number of workers varies from 3-5.
- ◢ Get a separate bid for packing services and moving services if you are undecided about packing yourself or having someone do it for you.
- ◢ Ask about insurance coverage for damaged items. Many companies will not insure items in boxes you pack yourself.
- ◢ Most movers do not show up on moving day with extra packing boxes. If you aren't packed up don't expect them to do it for you.

Check consumer websites like The Better Business Bureau, *www.bbb.org, troubleshooter.com* (free if you live in the Denver, Colorado or Houston, Texas metropolitan area) and/or Angie's List at *angieslist.com,* a paid subscription service for honest consumer feedback about the companies you are considering.

Protect Your Move

MOVING BELONGINGS FROM ONE PLACE TO ANOTHER is a risky proposition. If you hire a full service moving company you want your belongings to be fully covered for loss or damage. Below is information that explains some of the insurance options when you move.

Interstate Moving Companies Offer Two Types of Insurance

- ▲ **Full Value Protection.** Your mover is liable for the replacement value of lost or damaged goods in your entire shipment. The exact cost of this type of insurance varies from mover to mover. This is the default choice for all moves.
- ▲ **Released Value Protection.** There is no additional charge for this type of insurance but it covers no more than 60 cents per pound of article. For example, if you have an end table that weighs 100 pounds and a leg is broken off, you would receive $6.00 maximum reimbursement. You must specifically sign for Released Value Protection or you will be transported and charged for the Full Value Protection.

Other Insurance Tips

- ▲ Full Value Protection limits the amount you can claim on items of extraordinary value–items whose value exceeds $100 per pound–like jewelry, silverware, china, furs, and antiques unless you specifically list these articles on the shipping documents.
- ▲ You can purchase additional moving insurance for your belongings from a third party such as your own homeowner's insurance.
- ▲ Do not sign a delivery receipt for your household goods that contains language releasing your moving company from liability.
- ▲ By law, you have nine months to file a written claim. However, it is good practice to file a claim as soon as you are sure everything is unpacked and in good working order.
- ▲ Be aware of your deductible.

Actions that Limit Your Mover's Liability

- ▲ Packing perishable, dangerous or hazardous materials specifically prohibited by your mover.
- ▲ Packing yourself. While it will reduce your moving costs, it is more difficult to establish a claim for things that break during transit.

DIY Movers

- ▲ Make sure your homeowner's insurance covers your belongings during a move.

Appraisers

IF YOU HAVE HIGH-VALUE ITEMS IN YOUR HOME (art, furniture, collections, antiques, jewelry, etc.) obtaining an appraisal before a move is good insurance. If any of these items are lost or damaged during your move, you will be able to present this appraisal to the moving company or your homeowner's insurance agent for reimbursement.

Appraisers establish a "verifiable" value for an item or a collection of items. There are different values for insurance, estate tax, market value, auction value, or charitable contribution purposes. For people who are moving, an insurance value would be the appropriate choice.

Appraisers can range from informal, like a local antiques dealer, to a formal, certified, professional appraiser. An appraisal by a professional appraiser can be quite expensive, and only needed if the value of your item or collection is very high. If you think you have belongings that need an appraisal, consult with your insurance agent to discuss which type of appraisal is appropriate.

Questions for Appraisers

◢ **What are your credentials?** Are you certified by any national organizations? (A professional appraiser should have excellent credentials.)

◢ **Do you have specific expertise in my type of property?**

◢ **How do you establish your fees?** This could be an hourly rate, a flat rate or a "per item" rate.

◢ **What does your final report contain?** Formal appraisals should always include a typewritten report including: a cover letter with the date of appraisal, appraiser's qualifications, statement that he/she has no financial interest in the property and a signature. The report should list a complete and accurate description of each item with a defined value, and state the methodology used. Confirm that the appraiser will defend the report in court, if necessary. An informal appraisal should be written (and shown to your insurance agent to confirm it is adequate) and list each item and its estimated value.

Storage Units:
Consider the Costs

"STORAGE: THE EXPENSIVE WAY TO THROW SOMETHING OUT," says Don Aslett, author of *Clutter's Last Stand*. Most people put things into storage believing they will "get to it soon." Before they know it their things have been in storage for years, and they've paid thousands of dollars keeping it there.

Questions to Ask Before Putting Things in Storage
- ◢ Will I really use these things again?
- ◢ How long do I need to store them?
- ◢ What are my other options for dealing with these belongings?
- ◢ Are the items I'm storing worth the money I'm spending to store them?

Rental Costs Add Up:
$100/month storage unit rental x 1 year = $ 1,200
$100/month storage unit rental x 5 years = $ 6,000
$100/month storage unit rental x 10 years = $12,000

The following table shows average costs across the country for storage unit and POD type rentals. Rental costs are higher in urban areas and less in rural areas.

Average Monthly Rent for Storage Units

Size	What It Holds	Average cost
5' x 5'	Contents of small closet	$40-50/mo
10' x 10'	Contents of 1-bedroom apartment	$50-100/mo
10' x 15'	Contents of small 2-bedroom house	$75-140/mo $170-180/mo (climate control)
10' x 20'	Size of one-car garage	$90-150/mo
POD type portable unit (8' x 7' x 7')	Contents of bedroom	$230/mo

Options for Storage

Considerations

- ▲ What type of unit? The options are detailed below.
- ▲ Will you need easy access? Storage units located on the outskirts of a city are usually less expensive than close-in units, but might be less convenient.
- ▲ Will you need a climate-controlled unit? If you are storing fragile things with value like antiques, collectible books, linens, you should consider a climate-controlled unit, especially if you live in a hot, cold or humid climate.
- ▲ Will you need shelving? If you are storing items you will frequently access, you don't want to unstack and restack boxes all the time. Inexpensive shelving allows you to access frequently used items with ease.
- ▲ Do you want 24-hour access? Some companies offer this, some don't.

There are two types of storage most homeowners use, self-storage units (Ace and Public are examples of nationally franchised companies) and the new portable, self-contained units (PODS, Door-to-Door and PackRat, to name a few).

Factors to Consider When Selecting a Storage Unit System

Self Storage Unit	Portable Storage Unit
Wide variety of unit sizes available	Range from 5'x7' to 8'x15' (approximate)
Storage at their facility	Store at site of your choosing or their facility (community zoning laws apply)
Relatively easy access	Can't access if stored at their facility without incurring additional charges
Owner moves items to storage site	Pack on your property
Owner moves items out of storage unit to New home	Storage container delivered to your site of choice for unpacking.

You will also need to purchase a heavy-duty padlock. Make sure the storage company you hire provides 24-hour security and verify that your homeowners insurance protects your belongings while in storage.

To calculate more exactly how much storage space you need, try this useful online space calculator at *cudahyselfstorage.com/calculator.htm*.

Hiring a Real Estate Agent

WE ARE NOT REAL ESTATE AGENTS but we work with a lot of them. There are agents, good agents and great agents. Here's what we look for in a great agent.

Experience
This is not the time to give your best friend's son who is "breaking into the business" your listing. Experience in real estate does not just mean numbers of years working as an agent. Experience is about how many homes an agent has sold and how many buyers they've helped.

Real Estate Agents with Connections
Connections are what it's all about. Great agents belong and participate in groups and organizations in their community. The more active your agent is in the community, the more likely the agent will come in contact with other agents who have a buyer for your home.

Companies with a Large Presence in Your Area
These can be nationally recognized companies or strong, locally based ones. Read the ads. Pay attention to "for sale" signs as you drive about town.

Recommendations
Ask your friends, colleagues and neighbors if they know of a top-quality agent. When you're interviewing agents, ask for a list of references and call them.

Real Estate Agents Who Talk Straight with You
Our favorite agent tells us, "I'm an expert at what I do." Your agent may recommend things you don't agree with (this often comes up with suggestions for decluttering, staging and pricing). You need to have confidence in the person you hire and take his/her advice.

Great Agents Keep in Touch with You
Find out how often your agent will communicate with you and if they give you feedback after every showing. Clients who are most satisfied with their real estate agents, even in slow markets, are those whose agent kept in regular contact with them.

Look for Agents with Helpful Resources
Realtors who go the extra mile have high quality, reliable referral lists. Preparing a house for sale usually means needing a wide variety of services. A good referral list will save you time.

Find Agents Who are Web Savvy
Agents who have a web presence with an easy-to-navigate website have a much greater pool of prospective buyers than agents who don't.

Mortgage Glossary

IF YOU ARE PURCHASING YOUR FIRST HOME you'll be amazed at the number of unfamiliar words people use when referring to mortgages, also called a home loan.

- ◢ **Fixed Rate Mortgage.** A fixed rate mortgage is a basic, straightforward loan that offers an interest rate that's fixed for the life of the loan. The same principal and interest amount is paid every month.
- ◢ **Adjustable Rate Mortgage.** Interest rates for adjustable rate mortgages (ARM) change over time. Some people like these because they can get a lower interest rate and monthly payment in the beginning of the mortgage. After this, interest can go up or down, but can only go as high as the lifetime cap.
- ◢ **Interest-Only Mortgage.** A loan in which a borrower will only pay the interest for a certain period of time. After the interest only period is over, the borrower starts paying principal.
- ◢ **Interest Rate.** The annual fee for borrowing which determines the amount of interest paid at each monthly installment.
- ◢ **Annual Percentage Rate.** A more accurate expression of yearly cost of borrowing than just the interest rate, the APR takes into account interest, points, and other costs such as credit report fee, mortgage insurance, and origination fees. These costs are spread over the life of the loan.
- ◢ **Discount Points.** Interest charges paid up-front when a borrower closes a loan. Generally, by paying more points at closing, the borrower reduces the interest rate of the loan and thus future monthly payments.
- ◢ **Origination Points.** A fee (usually a percentage of the loan) imposed by a lender to cover certain processing expenses in connection with making a loan.
- ◢ **Mortgage Term.** The length of time it will take to pay the mortgage off. The longer it takes to repay the loan, the smaller each payment will be, but the loan will cost more because the borrower will owe more in interest. The less time it takes to repay the loan, the higher each payment will be, but the borrower will build equity faster.
- ◢ **Amortization.** Amortization is the paying back of money borrowed plus interest. The actual term, or length of the mortgage along with the amortization, is what determines what the payments will be and when the loan will be paid off.
- ◢ **Equity.** The difference between what your home is worth and the amount you owe on it.
- ◢ **Escrow.** A portion of the monthly payment in addition to the mortgage payment. This is used to pay property taxes and insurance premiums.
- ◢ **Closing Costs.** The money paid to complete your purchase. This includes money for legal fees, insurance fees, bank costs, property taxes and escrow.

Don't Become a Victim of Loan Fraud

WITH ALL THE HEADLINES IN THE NEWS recently regarding sub-prime mortgages, it is wise to make careful decisions when selecting a home mortgage. Even good people can make poor choices or get misled by an unscrupulous lender. Below are some warning signs to be aware of when shopping for a mortgage.

Tips for Selecting a Home Mortgage

- ◢ Always shop for mortgages.
- ◢ Be suspicious of anyone who offers a "bargain loan."
- ◢ Avoid lenders who call and promise guaranteed, low-interest loans, take applications over the phone, or offer next-day approval if a down payment is made immediately.
- ◢ Get information about the cost of other homes in the area. Don't be fooled into paying too much.
- ◢ Make sure a home inspector is licensed and qualified. Agree in writing, whether the buyer or the seller is going to be responsible for paying for necessary repairs.
- ◢ Do not be persuaded to make false statements on your loan application, such as overstating your income or failing to disclose your debts.
- ◢ Do NOT let anyone convince you to borrow more money than you know you can afford to repay.
- ◢ Never sign a document containing blank lines.
- ◢ At closing, compare the loan application you submitted with the final loan application the lender gives you to sign.
- ◢ Understand the total cost of the loan.
- ◢ Make sure you understand the fees and other costs associated with your loan.
- ◢ Don't sign anything you don't completely understand.

Protect Your Security Deposit

IF YOU ARE MOVING INTO OR OUT OF A RENTAL UNIT, it is important to understand security deposits. A landlord requires a deposit to ensure you leave the unit in good condition. Unless you damage the property, this deposit is returned at the end of the lease. Use the following tips as a guide to protect your security deposit.

Moving In
- Before you move in, walk through the unit with the landlord. Write down any existing damage—they may have a form for this—both of you should sign and date the document. Don't forget to check things like the operation of appliances, water pressure and temperature of hot water and sink drainage.
- "Normal wear and tear" is a term commonly used in rental contracts. It is term that means different things to different people. Protect yourself—talk with the landlord to get his/her definition. Take pictures of anything you think appears worn.
- Use detail when describing existing damage. For example, don't say "stained countertop." Write "burn marks on the counter to the left of the sink."
- You and your landlord should keep your own copy of this check-in document.
- Use a check or money order with a duplicate stub to pay for the security deposit. A receipt signed by the landlord is also acceptable. In case of a dispute, you need a paper trail.

Moving Out
- Your rental property should be returned to the landlord clean. This means:
  - Floors swept and mopped, carpets vacuumed.
  - Drawers and cabinets emptied and cleaned.
  - Kitchens wiped down including the inside of the refrigerator, microwave and oven.
  - Bathrooms thoroughly cleaned; toilets, sinks and bathtubs, medicine cabinets and mirrors.
  - All trash removed from the property.
- Before you move out, schedule a walk-through with the owner or property manager. Ask what you need to do to get your deposit back in full. Write down the damages you are responsible to repair and have him/her sign the document. At this point you should be responsible for those specific repairs to get back your full deposit. Don't wait until the last minute to do the walk-through, allow time for making repairs.
- Don't forget to return the keys before you drive to your new home.
- Make sure your landlord has your new mailing address.
- Keep all contracts associated with your apartment until your security deposit check has cleared the bank.

Organizing for Your Move

Why Declutter Before a Move?

WE CAN GIVE YOU A MILLION GOOD REASONS to declutter and organize your home before you move. Lots of them have to do with making things easier for yourself and starting life in your new home clutter-free. But the real reason comes down to cold, hard cash.

You Won't be Paying to Move Things You Don't Want

If you are using a packing crew they will pack everything including the junk drawer full of broken rubber bands, random nails, and ancient gum. They'll pack the half bottle of lotion that's been in the bathroom for three years and your hall closet full of clothes you haven't worn since the 1980's. By not decluttering you not only pay the packers to pack your unwanted things, you pay the moving company to move it. Does that make sense? As a rule-of-thumb calculate that each small box that gets packed and moved costs you about $20.00.

Your Home May Sell for More Money

Decluttering your home so it shows better to prospective buyers is a great way to get top dollar for your home. If you are doing the packing yourself, using time and energy to pack things you don't want or need doesn't make sense.

Unpacking at Your New Home Will be Easier

You want your new home to feel fresh and clean. However, we've helped many people settle into their new homes who need a dumpster for the things they throw away. Over and over we hear people say, "Why did I move this?"

There are lots of reasons you should tackle the clutter and discard things you aren't going to want in your new home. But the number one reason to tackle the clutter? Your money. You should keep it.

The #1 money saving tip when you move is to sell or donate everything you don't use or need before you move!

Letting Go is Hard

CHANCES ARE, AS YOU SORT THROUGH YOUR BELONGINGS, you are going to find things that don't fit in the "love it" or "use it" category, but you can't imagine letting go of them. These are the things that clog the back of your closets or are in the boxes in the basement. Typically, it is a family heirloom that was passed down to you, a gift from someone you love, or a piece of your personal past. Here are some ideas to make it easier to let go.

I love Aunt Edna and don't want to hurt her feelings, but I never liked the replica Liberace piano she gave me...

Stop feeling guilty. Now is the time to discreetly donate the item (don't put it in your garage sale if there is a chance she will show up.) If Aunt Edna misses it, you can chalk it up to that one missing box or the unfortunate breakage that occurred.

It was my great-great grandmother's china...but we've never used it.

Family heirlooms are especially tough to deal with. A client had a beautiful way of dealing with her mother's china that sat in storage for years. She prepared one of her mom's legendary meals and served it on the china. The family talked about Grandma and the great meals she cooked for them. They took a group picture. Then they donated the china to a thrift store specializing in upscale items and bought a beautiful silver frame for the group photo. Now, they always remember their grandma and her china.

I can't send my high school letter jacket to the thrift store.

Theatre companies are frequently looking for clothing for their props department. If you have vintage clothing, costume jewelry, or old prom dresses/tuxedos, contact them to give your clothes a new life.

Making space in your life for new things that you love and use is one of the best things you can do for yourself.

Staging Strategies

PRESENTING YOUR HOME IN A WAY THAT IS APPEALING TO BUYERS is important to selling your home quickly and at top dollar. Statistics show that staged homes sell faster and for more money. Staging a home means making it look like a model home. There are three steps to staging.

- Cleaning and repairs
- Decluttering
- Furniture placement and accessorizing

Inside

- Your home should be squeaky clean. Now is the time to clean baseboards, vacuum spider webs and make your bathrooms gleam. Don't forget the top of the refrigerator, high ledges, and light fixtures.
- Paint can instantly freshen a room. Most stagers recommend neutral colors with maybe an accent wall or two. If you are uncomfortable about making paint color choices, ask your real estate agent for advice.
- Repair all the little things—leaky faucets, squeaky drawers, drywall stress cracks, broken window coverings, doors that don't close properly, etc.
- A little money goes a long way in updating your home's look. New knobs on cabinets, fresh curtains, new towels and upgraded light fixtures are examples.
- Look at the furniture in each room. Is there too much? A dining room that is hard to walk in because there is a table, a sideboard and a hutch will look much larger with just the table.
- The focal point in the living room should be the fireplace, not the TV.

Outside

- First, do a walk around your yard. Look at it with prospective buyer eyes. Remove lawn ornaments and other objects that distract from the lawn itself.
- Keep lawns neatly trimmed.
- Pull weeds and keep flowerbeds clean. Add flowering plants if the season allows. New mulch makes flowerbeds looks fresh.
- Keep sidewalks and driveways clear of leaves or snow.
- Prune trees of dead limbs.
- Wash windows.
- Prospective buyers will wait at the front door while their realtor unlocks the house. Front doors and porches should be especially clean and free of cobwebs. Flowering pots are a nice touch.
- Put the "For Sale" sign in a prominent place and keep the sales brochures box full.

Decluttering for Staging

WHILE IT IS EASY TO SEE WHAT NEEDS TO BE CLEANED OR REPAIRED IN A HOME BEFORE YOU SHOW IT, decluttering is more subjective. We've had many clients offended by professional staging advice. They were asked to remove the things they felt made their home special. That is the point. You want to remove the things that are special to you so buyers can imagine their own special things in your home.

Decluttering Tips to Stage Your Home Like a Pro

- Before any staging can start your home must be clean and clutter free.
- Family photos should be kept to a minimum. Take them down.
- Collections are distracting to buyers. You want the focus on your home, not your wine cork collection.
- Prospective homebuyers look inside closets and cabinets so these spaces should be cleared of things you don't use. Storage space is attractive to buyers. Make your closets appear spacious by packing off-season clothing.
- Kitchen counters should be cleared off. Limit yourself to two small appliances. Everything should be neatly in your cupboards.
- Bathroom toiletries should be stowed in cabinets and counters cleared.
- Home offices, especially if they are in a public area, should not have papers and office supplies on the desktop. Put staplers, pen cups and all other items in the drawers. If you have a tangle of cables in plain view, use cable management products for a more organized look.
- Bedside tables should hold a lamp and a clock. Put all other items away.
- Magazines and newspapers should be out of sight.
- Take a look at all your horizontal surfaces—tables, mantels, counters, etc. They should have the bare minimum of accessories. For example, the magazines, coasters, remote controls, and tissue box that usually live on the coffee table all need to go.
- Don't forget the garage. Buyers like to see a garage that can hold a car, not one that is stuffed with construction materials, sporting goods and gardening supplies. A wall storage unit can be used to hold these things.

Your Organizational Style

MOVING IS A GREAT TIME TO RETHINK your organizational systems. If you have a system that works, that's great. If you always struggle with organization, maybe you haven't found the right system.

Is It You or the System?

Many of the familiar systems for organizing are created by left-brained people who think in a linear way. Right-brained people are generally visually oriented and linear organizational systems don't work for them. To figure out what type of a thinker you are, answer the following questions.

Are You a Linear Thinker?

- Are your clothes lined up in the closet, facing the same way, even color coordinated with neatly lined up shoes?
- Does your kitchen counter have a coffee pot on it and not much else?
- Do you love a well-organized filing cabinet with typed labels? Does this system include hanging folders divided into major categories and sub-categories?
- Are your office drawers organized with dividers so every item has its own space?

Or a Visual Thinker?

- Are your clothes draped over your bedroom furniture?
- Do you have piles of paper all over the house?
- Do you like to be able to see everything you own?

Embrace Your Own Organizational Style

If you are a linear thinker, your belongings are probably neatly arranged. Even if you are a linear thinker AND a clutterbug, the clutter is most likely behind cabinet or closet doors.

A visual thinker has a greater challenge when organizing. Since they are most comfortable when they can see their belongings, they need to find creative ways of storing things.

Tips for Visual Thinkers

Instead of:	Try this:
Bureaus or armoires in the bedroom	Open shelving for folded clothes—use clear plastic containers for small items.
Upper cabinets in the kitchen	Open shelving for dishes—you can even take the doors off cabinets.
Filing cabinets and drawer organizers	Use plastic stacking trays to contain piles of papers neatly. Binders stored on open shelves are also helpful. Use pen cups to hold pens, markers, scissors, etc.

Sorting Strategies

OUR CLIENTS OFTEN SAY DECLUTTERING AND SORTING BEFORE A MOVE is the hardest part of the moving process. It requires many decisions about what to keep, some difficult to make. In the end, the happiest people are the ones who stuck with it. Their homes showed well and their new home was filled with only the things they used or loved.

Prepare to Sort

- ◢ First, plan where you will put items you are going to sell, donate or store.
    - o If you are holding a garage sale, create a space in the garage to store all the sale items.
    - o If you are donating, get your trash bags and boxes ready. Make a plan to go to the charity at the end of the day or schedule a pickup.
    - o If you are selling items, have your consignment shops picked or your online accounts set up and ready for posting.
    - o If you need to store items for staging, have your packing materials ready.
- ◢ Get your sorting work surface ready. Large horizontal areas are best—a dining room or kitchen table, beds, folding tables. Pick the surface most comfortable for your back.
- ◢ Make sure you have bags for trash handy.

Like-With-Like Sorting

- ◢ We recommend sorting all like items at the same time, not room-by-room. For example, if your DVDs are stored with multiple TVs in your home, find every one of them and lay them out on your work surface to sort.
- ◢ Things that are often in more than one room are clothes, shoes, coats, books, DVDs, photos, medicines, first-aid supplies and toys.
- ◢ With this system, things that naturally get scattered throughout a house are now all together, you have sorted for what you want to keep, and everything is organized for packing. This is particularly helpful if you are a DIY packer.
- ◢ It is easy to get side tracked. Try to completely sort through one type of item before you move on to another one. For example, don't start searching for all the DVDs, see something that needs to be put away and then carry that to another room. By the end of this sorting process everything will be together and it is faster to concentrate on one item at a time.

Remove Unwanted Items Immediately

As you fill up a box for donation or sale, get it out of the house as quickly as possible. You'll be amazed at how good this makes you feel. If you are selling items online, create a space in your house where all those items are grouped together.

Cleaning Out Those Closets

CLOSETS COLLECT THINGS MYSTERIOUSLY. We frequently hear, "Where did that come from?" when we help clients go through their closets. Think forward to the closets in your new home—do you want your new closets overflowing too? Now is a great time to keep what you use and love and let go of the rest.

Linens

- A good rule of thumb is two sets of sheets for each bed you have.
- People often have an abundance of towels. Send stained and torn towels to the rag bag.
- If you use tablecloths and napkins sort through these, too. Many people change their entertaining style over the years and add to their table linens without removing the ones they no longer use.

Clothes

- Inspect your wardrobe. Anything stained or torn should be thrown away.
- If you have clothes that need mending or an alteration, get them to your alteration shop or dry cleaners.
- Now you're down to size and style. The best hint is: if you haven't worn it in a year, toss it. Many people keep the "size bigger and size smaller" clothes. Not a bad idea, but you should put clothes beyond that range in the sell/donate pile.
- If you have a lot of clothes, pack off-season clothes so your closets appear more spacious to prospective buyers.
- Repeat the same process with shoes, purses and accessories.

Bathroom

- Medicines first. Throw away anything that has expired (don't flush, it's bad for the water supply system). Next, sort and throw away ones you don't use or need.
- It's likely you will find gift soap, bubble bath and the like that you never use. Give them away.

Hallway/Miscellaneous

- Hallway closets collect things that belong somewhere else. Pull everything out. Sort through the coats, umbrellas, boots, etc. and put unneeded items in the sell/donate pile. Return misplaced items to their proper place.

See *Closets That Work* (p. *79*) for ideas on setting up closets in your new home.

Sorting the Kitchen

ALL KINDS OF UNUSUSAL THINGS WIND UP IN KITCHEN DRAWERS. A well-organized kitchen is a great place to be, so start your new home on the right track by sorting through your kitchen and eliminating the things you don't use.

Consider your cooking/entertaining/eating style. Has it changed or evolved? Let your current lifestyle dictate what you choose to keep.

Kitchen Sorting Tips

▲ If you don't know what the gadget does, you don't need it.

▲ Pull out all your pots and pans. Donate/sell the ones you don't use. Scratched Teflon-coated pans are a health hazard—throw them away.

▲ Assemble all of your glassware, including coffee cups. Most people have mismatched glasses, cups and mugs. Decide what you like (and use) and put the rest in the sell/donate pile.

▲ Food storage containers are another clutter area. Anything without a lid should be thrown away. If you have a mismatched collection that takes up space, toss it and get a new set. Ziploc and Glad make great nesting sets for less than $20.

▲ Utensils and gadgets quickly get out of control. Put everything out on the counter and survey the goods. Group like with like. Do you have five garlic presses? Why? Keep your favorites. Donate/sell the extras.

▲ Small appliances—this one is easy. Do you use it? If not, get rid of it.

▲ The junk drawer has a home in every kitchen. Some organizing experts say we don't need one; that it's just a place full of things we don't like to put away. We disagree. The kitchen is a great place for frequently used things that you want at your fingertips. Rid your junk drawer of things you don't use, broken things, and return things that belong elsewhere to their proper home.

▲ Don't forget food in the cabinets. If it has been there for over a year, or has an expired date on the product, throw it out. This especially goes for herbs and spices.

For kitchen design ideas in your new home, see *Setting Up Your Kitchen* (p. 78).

Clearing Out the Garage

AH, THE GARAGE! The place you discover things you never knew you owned. You may need to use your garage to store packed boxes or fill it with things for your garage sale. At a minimum you need to clean it out so it will show well to prospective buyers.

Have a Trash Plan

▲ Garage clean-outs generate lots of trash. Figure out your trash disposal system and have heavy-duty trash bags on hand.

▲ If you have an over-stuffed garage and large items to throw away, we highly recommend a dumpster.

▲ Chances are you will find old paint, fertilizers and weed killers you don't use. Movers will not pack or transport these things. Check with your municipal hazardous waste disposal program and dispose of these items responsibly.

Remove Everything

▲ While it may seem extreme, the best way to clean out a garage is to remove every single item in it. Pull everything into the driveway in groups—gardening supplies, sporting goods, tools, stored items, etc.

▲ When everything is out of the garage, sweep the floor. If you are working on staging your home for prospective buyers consider a fresh coat of paint on the walls. If part of your staging includes new shelving, install that now.

▲ Make a plan for placement of items that will go back into the garage, keeping like items together. If you store packed boxes or garage sale items in the garage, make sure you plan for that area, too.

Sort, Sort, Sort

▲ Remember, anything you keep you will need to move. If your garden hoe is dull and the handle is falling off, it makes more sense to toss it and buy a new one.

▲ Sort the items in each group you created. Put your keepers in one pile, donate/sell items in another and put the trash in your designated trash area. If you are a DIY packer now is the time to pack items you are keeping but won't need before moving.

▲ If you have boxes of memorabilia stored in your garage, open them. Many people move boxes from one house to another and have no idea what's in them. Only keep the things that are important to you.

▲ Move everything you are keeping into its designated new area in the garage.

Get your new garage off to a great start with *The Well-Organized Garage* (p. 81).

Toys, Toys, Toys

MOVING IS THE TIME TO get your kids' toys under control. We recommend a toy strategy that gets the toy clutter out of every room in the house. It allows kids to realize they really DO have too many toys, and it gets the broken ones, the ones they've outgrown and the ones they will be keeping sorted quickly. This strategy starts with getting all the toys in one room.

Step-by-Step Guide to Sorting Toys

◢ Create a toy staging area. If you have a lot of toys, select a large room to work in. Push furniture out of the way. Have trash bags on hand for trash and things to donate/sell. We use white bags for trash and black for donation or selling.

◢ Create sorting zones. Make signs and designate an area to sort the toys as they come in. Obvious signs are board games/puzzles, art supplies, books, etc. Don't forget the trash and donate zones.

◢ Bring in the toys. Make it fun! Offer prizes to the kid who finds the oldest toy, the dirtiest toy, etc.

◢ Eliminate the obvious. Broken toys, puzzles and games with pieces missing and mostly used art supplies go straight to the trash.

◢ Gently used toys the kids have outgrown or don't want go into donate/sell bags.

◢ With all the toys in front of you, pick a sorting strategy:
   o Keep one, give one away.
   o Here's four (or three or five) boxes—you can keep as many toys as fit in those boxes.
   o Have you played with it in the past 6 months? If not, let's donate/sell it.

◢ There are some toys the kids have outgrown that they want to keep. Create a keepsake box for each child for toys they (and you!) can't bear to part with. A plastic bin with a snug fitting lid works well. Label the bin with the child's name, and store it in the closet of their room or other storage area. If space is tight, use the "must fit in the box" strategy to limit how much they can keep.

Now you have the toys down to "the good stuff." If your move is soon and you are packing yourself, pack most of the toys. If a moving company is packing for you, put the toys neatly in their appropriate place.

Sorting Your Paper Clutter

ORGANIZING ALL THE PAPERS THAT COME INTO YOUR HOME is not easy. As we discussed in *Your Organizational Style* (p. 25), selecting a system that works for you is important. Here are some other tips to help you tame the paper clutter.

Sorting for Your Move

▲ **Gather the Easy Stuff.** Start where you keep the most papers. Create category piles and sort.

▲ **Search the House for More.** Many people have papers in the kitchen, papers in the office, papers in the bedroom. Before a move, you want to get them all in the same place for a thorough sort.

▲ **Only Keep What You Need.** Use our *Documents to Keep* (p. 91) checklist as a guide for what to keep and what to shred or recycle.

Suggestions for Your New Home

▲ **Think About What You Have Left.** These papers need an organization system that will work for you in your new home. Now is the time to make a change if change is needed. If you're not happy with your system, research ways other people have had success.

▲ **Trap Incoming Paper Clutter.** One of the best ways to keep paper clutter out of your new house is to prevent it from getting past the entryway. Keep your paper recycling bin close to the door and, on your way inside, take a minute to toss junk mail and unwanted catalogs. (For security, pass credit card offers and financial solicitations through a shredder.)

▲ **The Scanner is Your Friend.** Paper documents can be scanned and stored digitally. Use a scanner and digital filing system can cut your paper storage needs in half.

▲ **Different Types of Papers Need Different Systems.** If you clip lots of articles you intend to read or love clipping recipes for future use, come up with a system that makes it easy for you to keep those papers in one place. For papers that you don't access very often, like instruction manuals or warranty cards, binders or file folders make sense.

▲ **Store It Where You Use It.** If you love take-out, organize your menus in a three ring binder or a clear envelope in the kitchen. Keep a nice basket or decorative box in the room where you read magazines to keep them off the tables and floor.

▲ **It's Not Just Your Filing System.** More than one person in your family may need to touch some papers every day, like kids' school assignments. Make sure everyone is aware of the expectations of getting papers to the correct spot.

Organizing Your Photos

GET YOUR PHOTO COLLECTION INTO ORDER with these quick tips. This is not about creating scrapbooks or cropping photos. It's about getting all your photos together to organize and consolidate them. If you get the family involved, it can be fun!

Supplies

- **Photo boxes.** Find them at hobby shops, Target, Wal-Mart, specialty camera stores or online, usually for under $10. We use two types:
    - Photo storage boxes. Usually about 6 1/2" x 9 ¼" x 5 ¾". These are perfect for storing photos still in their envelopes and CDs.
    - Scrapbook cases (12" x 12" x 3") are perfect for oversized photos that need to lie flat.
- **Post Its.** Use for temporarily labeling boxes while you are sorting.
- **Archival quality black pen or #2 pencil.** Best for quick labeling of photos.
- **Index cards (4" x 6").**

The Quick Sort and Store

- Gather all your photos together. The dining room table is a good surface to work on. If the photos are in their photo finishing envelopes keep them there for now.
- Divide and stack the photos in categories. Here's an example of categories for a married couple with kids:
    - husband and his family before marriage
    - wife and her family before marriage
    - married life before kids
    - married life after kids
    - miscellaneous
- Take each stack and arrange it into general chronological order.
- Throw away the bad photos. Be tough—no blurry ones, none with eyes closed, none that are simply bad.
- Put the photographs into a storage box. Label dividers (if your boxes didn't come with enough dividers, use 4x6 index cards) by category and chronological order and put photos into their place.

Do You Need a Dumpster?

WHEN YOU MOVE, SOMETIMES IT'S COST EFFECTIVE TO RENT A DUMPSTER to haul your trash away. This is particularly true if you have large items you need to dispose of. Then, as long as you have it, you can throw the small stuff in too. The nice thing about a dumpster is that you can get bulky trash items out of your house quickly and not have to worry about repeatedly arranging for trash hauling.

Determine if You Need a Dumpster and the Size You Will Need

Our first rule of thumb is to estimate what you think you'll need and rent a size bigger. It is always less expensive to pay for the one-time dumping of a larger size than to pay for multiple dumps of a smaller one.

Estimating Your Trash

Go through your house room-by-room and make a list with rough measurements of things you need to throw away:

- ◢ Old couches and broken furniture
- ◢ Mattresses (it is extremely hard to give away mattresses)
- ◢ Broken down patio furniture
- ◢ Yard debris (try recycling options first)

Add up the sizes of the largest and bulkiest of these items to determine the minimum size dumpster you will need. A 5' x 6' x 5' container will barely fit a 6' couch and it takes up about 1/3 of the space. A twin-sized mattress and box spring will take a quarter of the space. Note that trash in roll-offs must be level with the top of the container.

After you determine the amount of space you need for your biggest items, make your best estimate for additional trash. If you haven't moved or conducted a good clean-out in a long time, chances are you will generate a significant amount of trash.

Pack the Container Efficiently

After you get your big bulky items into the dumpster be sure to pack trash into the airspaces surrounding them. People tend to toss trash into roll-offs thinking there is limitless space. Save yourself additional hauling charges by using all the available space.

Be Proactive

Your neighbors may consider your dumpster a community service and try to put their unwanted things into it. Post a large "No Dumping" sign to let them know it is off limits.

There are many important restrictions on what can be put in a dumpster. Check with your rental company for details about your area regulations.

Trash and Recycling Options

YOU'VE RECYCLED, YOU'VE DONATED, YOU'VE SOLD THINGS and still you'll generate trash. The cost of trash removal is becoming more and more expensive. In our experience people underestimate the amount of trash they'll generate during a move and pay more than they need to for removal services.

To save money, explore options. Read *Do You Need a Dumpster? (p. 33)* to help you calculate how much trash you'll generate. Often renting a dumpster is less expensive than having multiple smaller trash pickups.

There are three general types of trash removal services and many companies offer a combination of these services:

Garbage Collection/Waste Management
These terms refer to contractors in your area that provide weekly trash collection. In some towns waste management is part of city services. Most waste management companies offer a variety of services including dumpster rentals, recycling, one-time special pickup, hazardous waste drop off sites and more. Call or visit the website of your local providers.

Haulers
Trash haulers haul trash you set in a driveway or easily accessible outdoor area of your home. Few haulers come indoors. One nationally based franchise that removes things from *anywhere* in your home is 1-800-GOT-JUNK? Some haulers are environmentally friendly and recycle as much as possible. If this is important to you, ask their policy.

Dumpsters and roll-off rentals
The terms dumpster and roll-off are used interchangeably. Dumpsters come in a wide variety of sizes. The rental company will advise you on the appropriate size. Roll-offs are usually rented for a fixed period. Your cost estimate should include delivery, pickup and disposal. Negotiate for the time period you think you'll need the dumpster. It's convenient to have a dumpster on-site for the duration of the house clean out.

Because of seasonal demands for dumpsters, they may be more expensive or unavailable in the summer. Certain items may not be placed in dumpsters. Your rental company will provide you with a list. Most cities have regulations that prohibit placing dumpsters on the street. Check your city's regulations.

Recycling
More and more communities offer a wide range of recycling options. The National Recycling Coalition at *nrc-recycle.org* has a national database of recycling services for communities across the country.

Donating and Selling

Donating

Sell It Yourself

Have Someone Sell It for You

Sell or Donate?

YOU CAN MAKE MONEY from selling your unwanted belongings but it will also take a lot of your time and energy. In our experience people tend to **overestimate** the money they will make and **underestimate** the time and energy it takes to make that money. Before you decide to sell, ask yourself these questions:

How Much Will You Really Make?

- In deciding how much an item is worth, remember it is what someone else is willing to pay, not how much it cost you.
- Look at your big-ticket items and determine a realistic asking price. Reduce that by 25% if you are selling it yourself. Reduce by 50-60% for commissions if you have someone sell it for you.
- The average garage sale makes less than $600 and takes 30 hours.

Do You Have the Time and the Energy?

- Unless you already know how to sell things on the Internet, be prepared to spend LOTS of time learning how to successfully do it.
- Tracking down consignment shops takes time. Unless you have a way of getting furniture to the shop expect a pickup charge.
- Answering phone calls or e-mails and showing items to prospective buyers when selling on *craigslist.org* or local classifieds can interrupt your day.
- Factor in your time online, buying packing supplies, packing and the trip to the post office when you think about posting something on eBay.

Do You Have a Thick Skin?

- Consignment shops won't take everything you offer them and people will pick through your things and ask for a discount at your garage sale. If you are easily offended think twice about putting your things up for sale.

Consider Donating

By carefully documenting your donation, you can get a sizeable tax deduction, and charities that pick up items make it quick and easy to clear your home of unwanted things. Just remember, they want usable items in good condition, not your trash.

Still Planning to Sell?

You may have a number of items that are saleable. We have great tips in the pages ahead to make those sales quicker and easier.

Donating Tips

WE LOVE DONATING. Everyone wins. In our experience people spend a lot of time trying to sell things they ultimately end up donating. These tips will save you time and get things out of your house efficiently.

Find One Place to Donate Everything

Save time by donating to the shop that accepts the widest range of items that you have to give.

Find a Charity that Offers Free Pick Up

Some charities will pick up your donation. **Save time** by finding one that comes to you.

Know Your Charity's Restrictions

Many do not take older appliances, sleeper sofas, mattresses, outdated computers and electronics. Charitable thrift shops are becoming particular about accepting worn and dated furniture. Check their website or call.

Determine Pick Up Guidelines

Many charities with pick up service only take items from a front porch or driveway. If you have furniture in your house you want them to take, **save time** by calling first. If you have a large number of items tell the scheduler in advance. You don't want to be at the end of a route and find there is no room on the truck.

Schedule Ahead for Pick Up

Schedule your pick up. Most charities have specific schedules to best use their limited resources. Don't expect to call and have a truck arrive a few hours later.

Be Reasonable

Only donate items that are in good condition. Torn or stained clothing, electronics that don't work, puzzles with missing pieces and broken toys are not good donations. It takes time and effort for the charity to dispose of items that are not in good condition.

Time and Money Saving Tip: If you have furniture to donate on upper or lower levels of your house, have your movers put it in your garage and arrange for a charity pick up after the movers leave.

Charitable Donations—
Get Your Write-Off

MANY PEOPLE FIND PREPARING TO MOVE the perfect time to give away things they don't need or use any more. If you itemize your deductions on your tax return, taking some time to document your donations will pay off when the tax bill comes.

Documenting Donations

The IRS has tightened regulations on charitable donations. Deductions may only be taken on items that are in "good used condition or better." To ensure you receive the full value of the donation, we recommend you log each item you donate and, if possible, take photographs.

For example, if you are emptying a closet, lay all the clothes on the bed and take a photograph before putting them into bags or boxes. You don't need to take individual photographs of every item; you need to give someone looking at the picture a sense of how many items and their general condition.

If you are donating a large number of items or things of high value, contact your tax attorney, accountant or financial planner to confirm that your recordkeeping is adequate. IRS Publication 526, Charitable Contributions, contains detailed information on contributions at *irs.gov/publications/p526/index.html*.

Calculate the Deduction

Fair market value can be determined in various ways:

- ◢ Visit a charity thrift store and see how they price their items.
- ◢ Charity Deductions at *charitydeductions.com* is a web-based program specifically designed to provide valuations of charitable tax deductions.
- ◢ A general rule of thumb is if the item is in good condition you can use 25% of its purchase price as fair market value.
- ◢ Check online valuation guides like *satruck.com/ValueGuide.aspx* from the Salvation Army.
- ◢ Ask your financial planner or accountant for advice.
- ◢ There are specific and separate rules for valuing vehicles. Information can be found at *irs.gov/pub/irs-tege/pub4303.pdf*.

How to Hold a Successful Moving Sale

MOVING SALES ARE A QUICK WAY to get extra cash in your pocket and clear things out of your home. However, people tend to underestimate the time it takes. Most sales make less than $600 unless you have large ticket items (like cars or appliances.) Here are the steps to take for a successful sale:

Sorting/Staging
- ◢ Select a staging area.
- ◢ Group items by type. Have enough tables to display grouped items together.
- ◢ Clothing sells best when clearly labeled by size.
- ◢ Clean items sell faster. Clean as you go (dust or wash). Press wrinkled clothes/linens.
- ◢ Think of your moving sale as a retail store. Arrange items attractively.
- ◢ As things sell continue to rearrange and display items.

Pricing
- ◢ Visit local garage sales to get a feel for pricing.
- ◢ Start pricing when you have items grouped.
- ◢ If you are running a 2-day sale mark things a little higher the first day and then mark them down the second.
- ◢ Seasonal items that can be used immediately will sell for more.
- ◢ During the sale, continue to evaluate your pricing. Your goal is to sell things. Use a red marker and drop prices as the day goes on.

Advertising
- ◢ Start advertising your event 2-3 days in advance. Lead off with MOVING SALE or ESTATE SALE. List interesting or unusual items.
- ◢ Post an ad on Craigslist.
- ◢ Make large signs with high contrast colors on sturdy paper. The morning of the sale, post them at major intersections leading to your home.
- ◢ Do everything you can to make your sale feel welcoming. Tie a big bunch of balloons to large signs on your lawn or driveway. Create an attractive display of things you are selling at street level that draws people in.

Selling on eBay

EBAY PUTS A WORLD OF BUYERS AT YOUR FINGERTIPS. On the eBay website, you post an item for sale (usually with a photograph), someone purchases it, pays for it and you ship it out. eBay is a great place to sell things, especially collectibles.

However, the learning curve to set up an account is steep. If you have never used eBay before, count on spending 4-8 hours to get your first item online. This may be more time than you want to spend before moving.

Steps to Selling on eBay

1. Create an eBay account.
2. Set up a PayPal account to receive payments.
3. Photograph each item and upload to your computer.
4. Create listing, including setting minimum bid price and shipping charges.
5. Monitor your account frequently.
6. When it sells, package and ship item.

Tips for Selling on eBay

◢ Seek help. If you know people who sell on eBay, get their advice.

◢ Learn all you can about selling on eBay. There is a great tutorial on the eBay website. There are also many books on the subject.

◢ Don't bother with items that sell for $20 or less.

◢ Make sure your stated shipping and handling price includes cost of shipping, boxes and packing materials.

◢ eBay is a gamble. Setting a minimum bid helps ensure an item won't be sold for less than it is worth, but getting top dollar is never guaranteed.

◢ Be timely. Make sure you respond to inquiries and ship quickly. Customer feedback is an important part of eBay and you want customers to be satisfied with your service.

Resources for Selling on eBay

◢ *ebay.com* (Click on the "sell" button at the top of the page to learn more about their selling process.)

◢ *eBay for Dummies* by Marsha Collier

Selling on Amazon

AMAZON IS A GREAT PLACE to sell newer books, music CDs and DVDs. If they already list the item, you can sell it in the Amazon Marketplace. When an Amazon customer searches for an item, there is an option to purchase it used. You can sell anything that Amazon sells but books, CDs and DVDs are the easiest to pack and ship.

Selling on Amazon

- ◢ Set your sales price by looking at how much other people are asking for the same item. Amazon automatically adds a standardized shipping cost to the sales price, so you don't need to calculate the shipping.
- ◢ When your item sells, print out the packing slip and mailing label from the Amazon website and mail the item within two business days of the sale.
- ◢ Amazon collects the money from the customer, takes a commission and deposits the balance in your checking account.

Tips

- ◢ Make sure your sales price is worth your time and effort. There are many stores who sell things on Amazon that are content to make one dollar on a sale. A good rule of thumb is if you can't make $5 on something after Amazon takes its commission, donating that item makes more sense.
- ◢ Have your packing supplies on hand and mail items promptly.
- ◢ Remember, your time is going to get precious the closer you get to your move. Added trips to the post office can become burdensome.
- ◢ Amazon lists items automatically for one month. Remember to remove all unsold items and donate them with time to spare before your move.

Resources for Selling on Amazon

- ◢ *Amazon.com* (Click on the "Sell on Amazon" button at the bottom of the homepage.)

Selling on Craigslist

CRAIGSLIST IS A WEBSITE where you place local classified ads at no cost. You can list practically anything on this website. Additionally, if there is something you simply want out of your house or yard, post it in the FREE category.

Here's the Way It Works:

- ◢ To figure out a sales price, go to *craigslist.org*. Select your closest geographic area and do a search for the item you are selling. Notice which titles catch your interest and which ads you find most appealing. Listings that are clear, concise, name a price and include pictures are more successful.
- ◢ Post your item—we recommend photographing the item and uploading it, but that is not required.
- ◢ You receive an anonymous reply e-mail address so you do not need to include any personal information in your listing.
- ◢ Prospective buyers will contact you for more information and to set up a meeting time if they are interested. (See security concerns below.)
- ◢ Craigslist does not charge any fees or commission; the entire sales price comes back to you.
- ◢ It's a good idea to accept only cash for Craigslist sales. If you receive a bad check there is no middleman to help you get your money.

Security Issues

Security issues arise when selling items on Craigslist, newspaper classifieds, or grocery store message boards.

- ◢ Never put your address in an ad.
- ◢ If possible, use a cell phone for receiving calls. They typically cannot be traced back to a specific address.
- ◢ Never be alone when someone comes to look at an item.
- ◢ If the item is small, pick a public place to meet anyone who is interested in buying it. Meeting places might be a church (when lots of people are around), a grocery store parking lot, or a shopping mall. Bring a friend.

Resources for Selling on Craigslist

- ◢ *craigslist.org/about/help*

Hints for Selling on Consignment

THE MAIN ADVANTAGES to selling on consignment are:
- ◢ You get the item(s) out of your house.
- ◢ The shop does the advertising and selling for you.

Keep in Mind
- ◢ Consignment commissions range from 40%-60% of sales price.
- ◢ Factor in the cost of getting furniture to the store as most shops charge for pick up. If your profit is small, consider donating. You will help a charity and get a tax write-off.
- ◢ Most consignment shops donate unsold items to local charities. If you want unsold items back, make arrangements with the shop.

Furniture Consignment Shops
Don't show up at a consignment shop with a truckload of things thinking they'll take it all. Successful consignment shop owners know what sells and are selective about what they accept. Many have their own niche. In our town we have three furniture consignment shops. One accepts eclectic, funky pieces. Another specializes in furniture for the college crowd and the third in antiques.

Clothing Consignment Shops
Clothing shops also specialize. There are vintage shops, costume shops, stores that only accept designer labeled clothing, etc. As a rule, clothing must be clean, pressed and in excellent condition. Just because you have a brand-new item with the price tags attached does not mean a shop will take it.

Time Saving Tips
- ◢ A little homework will save you time and aggravation. Call and speak with the staff. Find out what items the store accepts.
- ◢ Ask stores if they do initial assessments from photographs. Many are starting to do this as a time saver.
- ◢ Many consignment store owners will come to your home if you have several things you'd like to sell.

Selling Through an Antiques Dealer

IF YOU HAVE ANTIQUES OR COLLECTIBLES that you are interested in selling, antiques dealers are a good resource. They can give you an informal estimate of an item's value and/or purchase the items.

Some dealers are certified appraisers, others are simply knowledgeable about the type of antiques they buy and sell. Some dealers purchase a wide variety of things while others specialize in specific collections like stamps, coins, silver, glassware or china. They may offer to purchase individual items or entire collections.

If an antiques dealer is purchasing items from you it is so he/she can resell the item. Selling to an antiques dealer is similar to selling an item at a wholesale price. The advantage to using an antiques dealer is that the transaction takes place quickly. The dealer purchases the items from you and takes them away. In contrast, it can take weeks to complete estate sales, auctions or on-line sales.

Tips

◢ Antiques dealers don't have a specific trade organization. Finding a reputable dealer takes research.

◢ Many larger towns have an "antiques row" area, a concentration of antiques shops and dealers. Walking from store to store and asking questions is a great way find a local dealer. Indoor flea markets are another good resource.

◢ Use Google to find dealers who sell on the Internet and are located in your area. Google "antiques dealers (name of city and state)." For example, "antiques dealers Boulder Colorado" should turn up dealers in Boulder.

If you have antiques or collectibles you need to sell quickly, an antiques dealer is a great way to go. You will not get top dollar, but you will save time and energy.

Using an eBay Trading Assistant

IF YOU LIKE THE IDEA of selling things on eBay but don't want to go to the effort of listing, tracking and shipping the items yourself, consider using a registered eBay Drop Off Location or Trading Assistant. These are companies or individuals that operate independently as eBay sellers and can sell your items for a fee or commission. Visit *ebaytradingassistant.com/directory/index.php.* on the eBay website for information.

Registered eBay Drop Off Locations: These are physical stores with regular business hours. You bring items you'd like to sell to the store. Generally an item must have a sales price of $50 or more for a store to accept it.

Trading Assistant: A Trading Assistant is an individual who usually operates out of his/her home. Many of these Assistants come to your home to assess your items. Trading Assistants work with you to set a sales price. They list the item and ship it to the buyer if it sells. They work on commission; their fees vary, but generally you can count on receiving about 50 - 60% of the sales price.

Questions to Ask

◢ **Are you experienced?** Get the store's eBay User ID and review their feedback response from buyers and length of time they have been selling on eBay. Don't use anyone with a positive feedback that is less than 98%. Check their current auctions. Look for good quality photos, informative and attractive layout and proper grammar.

◢ **Are you knowledgeable about the items you are trying to sell?** If the store does not have a lot of experience in the collectibles you are trying to sell, you need to know the fair market value of the items before you go to the store or find another eBay Assistant that does.

◢ **What are your fees?** Make sure there are no hidden charges.

◢ **Can I set a minimum bid?** If you do not set a reserve price, your item could sell for $1 and you would end up receiving almost nothing.

◢ **Will you charge you for unsold items?** eBay charges a listing fee for each item whether it is sold or not. Some will list your item again at no charge if it does not sell the first time.

◢ **What is the policy for unsold items?** If you have already moved, you may incur charges to have items shipped back to you if they have not sold.

Packing and Moving

New Home Projects to Complete Before You Move

MOST PEOPLE AREN'T LUCKY ENOUGH TO MOVE INTO A NEW HOME THAT IS EXACTLY PERFECT." Usually new homeowners have a punch list of tasks and home improvement projects they want done. We're not talking about major remodeling, but small jobs that will make your new home the way you want it.

Some of these jobs are easier to accomplish before you move in. If you have the luxury of time to work on your new home before you move in, put the following tasks at the top of your list.

- ◢ **Flooring.** Of all the changes to make before you move in, flooring is the biggest. Refinishing or installing a wooden floor or replacing carpet is best done in an empty house.
- ◢ **Interior painting.** Painters love working in an empty room, and can probably give you a lower bid if they are not working around furniture.
- ◢ **Closet organization.** If the closets have a single rod and you want a closet system installed, get that done before your clothes arrive. See *Closets that Work* (p. 79).
- ◢ **Appliance delivery.** It's easier to deliver and set up a washer/dryer or refrigerator in an empty house.
- ◢ **Garage storage.** Plan and install your garage storage before the bikes, sports equipment, gardening tools and workbench arrive. If you are bringing storage from your old home, make sure it gets loaded last so it can be unloaded first. See *The Well-Organized Garage* (p. 81).
- ◢ **Anything that involves sanding or scraping.** Sanding creates fine layers of dust that permeate everywhere. Flooring is the worst but if you want to sand the popcorn finish off the ceiling or put a darker stain on the kitchen cabinets, try to complete sanding and clean up before the move.
- ◢ **Re-keying the locks.** Who knows how many keys the previous homeowners gave out? For your safety, get a locksmith to re-key the exterior doors. Change the password to the garage door, too.
- ◢ **Media center wiring.** Complete any rewiring that is needed for your television, sound and computer systems.

Design Your New Home to Fit Your Lifestyle

DO YOU HAVE A ROOM IN YOUR HOME that is seldom used and other rooms that are bursting? Before you start putting your furniture into the "correct" rooms, we encourage you to stop thinking about room names and think about how you live.

Don't be afraid of this idea—the change doesn't need to be permanent. Joan's dining room has been a family office, a play room for the kids, a real dining room and now it is a living/dining/office combination. The room has changed to fit her family's current lifestyle. Here's some ideas for you to create the space you need.

Rethink Your Rooms

▲ **Create an office.** If you are tired of your home office being the kitchen table, take over an underutilized space and become more efficient and productive in the process.

▲ **Expand your crafty side.** Every time you get started on a creative project in the kitchen do you need to put everything away to serve dinner? Make a hobby room and let your creative side soar.

▲ **It's a playroom.** Young kids sometimes share a bedroom and if yours do, that frees up a bedroom to become a dedicated playroom for their toys.

▲ **Electronics central.** Convert a little used dining room into a media center for the kids. You'll see them more often, and be able to closely monitor TV and Internet usage.

▲ **Have fun.** If you keep your garage in good, clean condition use it for a party. Open the door, put up decorations, get some music going and you've got a party room.

▲ **Get some exercise.** Use a space to keep your New Year's resolution and eliminate the gym fees.

▲ **Teen social space.** The garage or dining room is also a place to put a pool table or ping pong table to give teens a space to entertain their friends.

Additional Ideas

▲ **Don't have an extra room?** Use visual room dividers to create a separate space. A decorative screen or handsome curtain hung from the ceiling can create a small area in a large family room for the office, exercise area or hobby room.

▲ **You don't need to eliminate your guests.** Keep a "guest room" in the closet. With a high quality inflatable bed, a small side table and a lamp at the ready, your guests can be comfortable for any short stay.

▲ **Need a dining room for the holidays?** Rearrange furniture in your living room or family room (even an entryway) for a holiday dining option.

Your Furniture Placement Plan

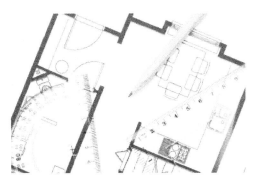

EVEN IF YOU ARE A DO-IT-YOURSELF MOVER, you need help moving heavy furniture into your new home. A furniture placement plan will save time and energy when you are directing where to place things at your new home.

Display the plan in a central area of the home or if you have drawn the rooms separately, post it on the wall in each room. When the movers arrive, make sure they see and understand the plan before they unload.

Reasons for a Plan

▲ **It saves you money.** If you have movers working at an hourly rate, wavering about where the couch goes while the movers are holding it and waiting for your answer costs you money, not to mention it makes the movers cranky.

▲ **It saves you energy.** If you don't know where the furniture should be placed, chances are the movers (even if they are your friends) will just plop it down anywhere. Then the rearranging is your problem.

▲ **It makes you aware of furniture you don't need or can't use.** This can save you money if you decide to sell or donate it instead of moving it.

Four Ways to Make a Plan

▲ Get a piece of paper, draw a rough estimate of the room, and sketch in where you think the furniture should go.

▲ If you want to be more precise, measure the rooms in your new home. Using graph paper, a ruler and a ¼" = 1' measurement, draw the room, and then the furniture where you want it located.

▲ Home design software, lets you play with floor plan designs on your computer.

▲ If you have blueprints, make a copy and sketch your furniture into each room.

Measure and Compare Before You Move

YOUR NEW HOME IS NOT GOING TO BE A CARBON COPY OF YOUR CURRENT HOME. You won't have the same amount or maybe even the same kind of storage space. Your large sectional may not fit down the stairs. To eliminate problems, plan ahead by measuring and comparing the two homes before you move.

While you are measuring and comparing, create a list of things you will need for your new home. The article *Organizing Supplies for Settling In* (p. 75) in the next chapter can help you identify needs.

Furniture

Stairways, narrow doors and tight corners can all cause problems.

- Measure any large furniture or appliances you will be taking with you.
- At your new home, measure your doors. This sounds like a no-brainer, but doorways come in a variety of sizes. You want to know if some of your furniture won't fit or will need to be brought in through a specific door. Taking a door off the hinge buys you an inch or two of extra width.
- Measure your stairway openings. Remember to measure the shortest distance from the stair treads to the ceiling above, too.
- Taking pictures will make your measurements clearer when you look at them later.

Kitchen

- Look at your cabinet and pantry space in both places. Will you need to rearrange where you store utensils, food and pots/pans? Are there amenities, like pull out shelves that you will not have in your new kitchen?

Clothes Closets

- Is your master bedroom closet bigger or smaller in your new home? If it is smaller, there are ways to deal with the downsizing.
  - o Downsize your wardrobe
  - o Use a guest closet
  - o Put a rolling rack in the basement for out-of-season clothes
- Will you need a closet organizer? If your new home only has the (extremely inefficient) builder's grade single rod and shelf, an organizing system will maximize your space.

Storage Closets

- Where are the closets in your new home? As you pack your closet contents to move, remember to label the boxes to reflect the storage in your new home.
- Make sure any storage containers you currently use fit into your new closets.

Make an "Open Me First" Box for Each Room

THERE ARE THINGS you use daily and will need immediately in your new home. It's important these things don't end up in the bottom of a box labeled "Miscellaneous" since you will want them the first night or next morning. Even if you are lucky enough to have a full-service move, you should pack these things in well-labeled boxes before the movers arrive to make sure you can find them easily in your new home.

Label the boxes with the room name and in LARGE letters "Open Me First" on all sides. The kitchen box can also be labeled "Please Put on Kitchen Counter" for added visibility. Below is a sample of items that should be in each box.

Bedrooms

- Sheets and pillows
- Kid's favorite toys/nighttime books
- Alarm clocks and bedside lamps
- Pajamas and a change of clothes

Bathrooms

- Toilet paper
- Towels
- Kleenex
- First aid supplies and medicines

Kitchen/Family Room/Utility Room

- Coffee pot, filters and coffee
- Set of plates, silverware, glasses, coffee cups
- Can/wine opener
- Snack food
- Paper towels
- Cleaning supplies
- Light bulbs
- Pet food
- TV remote controls
- Telephone and answering machine
- Cell phone chargers
- Tool kit. Make sure it contains at least two box cutters.

Things to Keep with You

THERE ARE IMPORTANT PAPERS AND IRREPLACEABLE ITEMS you should keep with you and not send on the moving truck. Whether you are moving across town or across country we recommend getting a banker's type filing box (the sturdy type with openings on each end for easy carrying) or a plastic carrying crate that's file-sized where you can keep your essential papers.

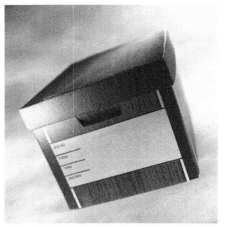

Types of Papers That Should Travel with You

We created a detailed list of essential personal and financial documents in the Checklists and Worksheets Section titled *Documents to Keep (p. 91)*. In addition to those documents, add these to your box:

▲ Moving workbook with all essential moving paperwork

▲ Current bills

▲ School records

▲ Pet records

▲ Address book

▲ Maps

▲ Phone book

▲ Back up disks of computer files

Valuables

▲ Jewelry

▲ Irreplaceable photographs, artwork, etc.

▲ Items not covered by moving insurance

Other Things to Bring with You

▲ Medications

▲ Keys

▲ Office supplies: paper, pen, pencil, tape, paperclips

▲ Box cutters

▲ Things not allowed in the moving van. See *Hazardous or Prohibited Items (p. 69)* for details.

Moving with Children

MOVING IS USUALLY NOT MOST KIDS' first choice. Change is difficult, and with kids it can be especially hard. Here are some strategies to help make moving less traumatic.

Play Up the Positive
If your kids no longer need to share a bedroom in your new home, that's a plus, as is a bigger backyard or a swimming pool close by. Teenagers may have their own bathroom. Make a list of the positives and post it on the fridge so they can be reminded it's not all bad.

Buy Something Special
That wished for xBox game, DVD or doll might be waiting for them in the new house if they have a positive attitude during the move.

It's Time for a Change
Maybe they've outgrown their room décor—give them a small budget and some direction to get the "big kid room" they've been wanting.

Make Time for Exploring
Unpacking can be time consuming and overwhelming, and after a move everyone is exhausted. While it might be hard, take time to check out the new neighborhood, find an ice cream shop, a great park, or other activity that your child loves.

Teenagers Have Unique Needs
Some teens find journaling their moving experience helpful. Some want a big going away party to connect with their friends before they leave. If your teen communicates with his/her friends through social networks like MySpace or Facebook, arrange for Internet service to be available as soon as you move in. Unpack the computer first so your teen doesn't feel disconnected.

Be Alert
Moving affects some children more strongly than others. Pay attention for subtle signs from your child that the move may be causing problems. Prolonged upset or moodiness shouldn't be ignored and may be a sign that extra support in adjusting to the move is needed.

Moving with Pets

IF YOUR PET WILL BE TRAVELING WITH YOU ON MOVING DAY take extra steps to ensure its safety. Moving is stressful for pets, too. Use the following guidelines for a successful pet move.

Tips for Dogs and Cats

◢ Schedule a pre-move health checkup with your vet. Make sure all vaccinations are current and carry proof of shots. If your pet needs to be sedated for the trip, order the drugs now. Update your animal's ID tag with your new home and phone information. Take a picture of your pet and note its size and weight. This is helpful if your pet gets lost.

◢ If you plan on driving and your pet is not accustomed to car travel, take it for some training rides before your trip.

◢ If you are driving, your pet travel kit should have water, food, bowls, can opener (if needed) leash, bedding, and poop bags or litter pan.

◢ Don't feed your pet for at least three hours before travel time. Take the dog for a vigorous walk before leaving.

◢ During stops, provide water, a brief walk and treats.

◢ Never leave any pet in a parked car on a warm day.

◢ You can find pet-friendly accommodations at *petswelcome.com*.

◢ During move-in, kennel your pet if possible. With so many access points in your home being open for movers, the chances of a pet slipping away are great. If a kennel is not an option, make sure the pet is in an escape-proof area, like a bathroom with a large sign on the door that says DO NOT OPEN or use a gate.

Flying with Pets

◢ Get a health certificate within 10 days of your travel.

◢ Make sure you are clear on all the airlines rules and fees. Confirm that your kennel crate meets airline specifications.

Tips for Small Animals and Birds

◢ Birds and small animals such as hamsters, gerbils or reptiles can usually travel in their cage during car travel.

◢ Birds and reptiles are susceptible to drafts and temperature changes. A cage covering during travel is recommended.

◢ Give all pets a chance to drink water at rest stops, especially during hot weather.

◢ Food can be given normally.

Moving with Plants

IF YOU HAVE PLANTS you have enjoyed and cared for over the years, you will want to ensure they arrive at your new home in good condition.

Before the Move

- ◢ If you are hiring a moving company, have them clearly outline their plant policy. Many companies do not move plants over 150 miles.
- ◢ If you have plants in heavy clay pots, transplant them into plastic containers and soil-less mix for the trip. (This makes the plant easier to move and the pot less likely to break.) Transplant well ahead of your move to allow the plant to recover.
- ◢ Check your plant for bugs, mildew or disease. If they need to be treated, consult your local nursery for advice on appropriate remedies.
- ◢ For larger plants, prune as needed to fit them into the box, car or van.
- ◢ The day before the move, water plants thoroughly.
- ◢ Plant cuttings are a great way to bring some of your old home to your new home. Take cuttings the day before you move. Wrap in wet peat moss or newspaper and place in unsealed zip top bags. Place upright in a box with packing paper for support to maintain moisture. Plant within several days of arrival.
- ◢ There is a special travel wrap used by nurseries for transporting plants. Contact your favorite nursery to learn how to get it.

Moving Day

- ◢ Pack plants last.
- ◢ Plants are susceptible to temperature changes. If it is cold and you are traveling overnight, bring them indoors. Intense sunlight through car windows burns plants.
- ◢ Don't put plants in the trunk of a car.
- ◢ Tall plants can be put in boxes for extra support. Cardboard flats are great for containing small plants and preventing spills.
- ◢ If the weather is warm, wrap damp newspaper around the plants to keep them cool on the road.

At Your New Home

- ◢ Unpack plants as soon as possible.
- ◢ Keep them out of direct sunlight for the first few days.
- ◢ Transported plants may be shocked for a while, but within a few weeks should be back to normal.

Helping Your Parents Move

AS ADULT CHILDREN, HELPING PARENTS MOVE FROM THEIR FAMILY HOME can be one of the most stressful moves of all. This move is frequently accompanied by a great sense of loss on the parent's part, and combined with the overwhelming number of decisions required to deal with all their personal belongings.

If considerable downsizing and passing on family heirlooms is a part of your move, we highly recommend the book *Who Gets Grandma's Yellow Pie Plate? A Guide to Passing On Personal Possessions.* This book is available through The University of Minnesota Cooperative Extension Service and on Amazon.

Making a Healthy Transition

▲ **Help Your Parents Choose the Best Living Situation.** Some will be moving to a smaller home to be near family. For others, senior communities that offer independent living, assisted living, or continuing care (CCRC) will be right.

▲ **Create a family plan.** Involve all family members from the beginning in decision-making. This goes a long way to minimizing hurt or angry feelings when it comes to dividing family heirlooms with either monetary or emotional value.

▲ **Honor the Memories.** Allow extra time, when sorting through photo albums and other memorabilia, to embrace the family history. You may hear stories you've never heard before.

▲ **Keep it Simple.** It may be too difficult for your parents to be present for all the sorting and downsizing. Keep this transition process as streamlined and easy on them as possible.

Help Is Available

▲ **Hire a Senior Real Estate Specialist (SRES).** This is a special designation for real estate agents who have completed classes that prepare them to approach mature clientele with the best options and information to make life-changing decisions.

▲ **Find a Senior Move Manager.** These companies help with the physical and emotional demands of later-in-life moves. From packing, overseeing moving companies, and settling in at the new home, they can do it all. If you want to do some or most of the work yourself, they offer a menu of services, from which you can choose and pay accordingly. Find one in your area at *nasmm.org.*

▲ **Hire an estate sale company.** This takes all the hassle of dealing with the personal possessions that won't be kept or passed on to family and friends. Most estate sales companies ask you to take everything you want out of the house, and then they come in and conduct a sale. They either charge a commission (usually a percent of sales) or add a premium to every item sold.

Planning Your DIY Move

MANY PEOPLE MOVE THEMSELVES. There are several things to start thinking about and many plans to be made. Be sure and read *Move Yourself or Hire the Pros* (p. 7) to explore your options.

Hire a Moving Truck

- ◢ You can hire a moving truck or a truck and moving crew. Reserve early so your truck is available exactly when you need it.
- ◢ Read *Hiring a Moving Company* (p. 10) in the first chapter for money-saving tips and strategies.
- ◢ Ask about hidden charges (one way trips, overtime labor charges, etc.) on your estimates that could throw your comparisons off. If you're hiring a smaller truck that will make multiple trips, remember to include the extra gas and mileage charges.
- ◢ If you plan to rent and drive a truck yourself, make sure you are comfortable driving it and confirm that a regular driver's license is adequate.
- ◢ Be clear with the moving company about long driveways, extra stairs and other unique situations that might add to your costs (both at your current home and your new one.)
- ◢ Check with your insurance agent. Understand your coverage while driving a rental truck and how your belongings are covered during a move. Learn about liability coverage in case anyone helping you gets injured.

Get Packing Materials

- ◢ Read *Good Deals on Packing Materials* (p. 60) to help you save money.
- ◢ Get new or used **moving** boxes. Packing is easier with uniform sized boxes. These boxes load efficiently in a moving van and reduce the likelihood of shifting which is the number one cause of breakage during a move.
- ◢ Create a staging area in your home where packed boxes can be stored, A cleaned and decluttered garage is a logical choice.

Schedule Manpower

- ◢ If friends offer to help, make sure they know the specific dates and times.
- ◢ If you need extra help, Craigslist is a great resource for finding day labor.

Be a Packing Pro

- ◢ The day before you move, have everything packed except the last minute items.
- ◢ Read our series of packing tips articles, we promise they will save you time.
- ◢ Throw a packing party—if you have all your supplies and instructions on hand it will make the job easier.

Good Deals on Packing Materials

THE FIRST THING MANY PEOPLE DO when they know they are moving is to start collecting boxes from grocery stores. While this may seem like a money saver, our experience shows you will save time, energy and money by using standard shaped boxes designed for moving because:

- ◢ Standard sized boxes stack compactly. This saves space in the moving van and allows your movers to load faster.
- ◢ Moving boxes are stronger.
- ◢ Using moving boxes is time efficient. You don't spend time searching through a stack of assorted box shapes to find one that suits your needs.
- ◢ Good moving boxes can be sold after your move to help you recoup some costs.
- ◢ Your time is valuable and making multiple trips to stores to find boxes is an inefficient use of your time.

Reduced Cost or Free Moving Boxes and Packing Paper

- ◢ You can frequently find free or reduced cost moving materials at *craigslist.com*. **TIP:** free boxes are snapped up quickly. You will have to monitor the site frequently and respond immediately to get your boxes.
- ◢ *Freecycle.org* is another online community to find moving boxes.
- ◢ If you are using one, check with your moving company. Some offer free wardrobe boxes if you unpack and return them before the truck leaves.
- ◢ Call a local realty company or your favorite real estate agent. Ask if they know of anyone who recently moved and has boxes available.
- ◢ *Usedcardboardboxes.com* offers used moving boxes and free shipping.
- ◢ U-Haul also has a box exchange. From their home page at *uhaul.com*, click on "Boxes" under "Moving Supplies." On the Boxes page, click on "Box Exchange."
- ◢ Your local recycling center may have used moving boxes.
- ◢ If you purchase moving boxes, ask if you can return unused boxes for a refund.
- ◢ See if there is a plastic box rental company in your area. In southern California *earthfriendlymoving.com* rents plastic boxes. They deliver and then pick up after you've moved.
- ◢ When contacting someone about boxes, ask for used packing paper, too.
- ◢ Call your local newspaper and ask if they have end-bolts of clean newsprint.

Your Packing Supply Kit

Boxes & Packing Materials

- ◢ **Moving boxes.** Small to medium boxes are the size of choice.
- ◢ **Packing paper.** Use clean newsprint for wrapping fragile items and things that need to be kept clean.
- ◢ **Packing tape.** Cheap tape is not worth the few dollars you'll save. It takes about 10 rolls to pack a 1000 square foot apartment.
- ◢ **Stretch wrap.** Also called "movers wrap," this plastic wrap sticks to itself and holds things in place without leaving any sticky residue. Use the 5" wide size (it looks like a lint brush roller) to hold drawers in place on small boxes, curio cabinets with unbreakable contents, and to keep things with several pieces together.
- ◢ **Bubble wrap.** Protects very fragile items.
- ◢ **Labels.** Large (3 1/3"x4") white mailing labels on boxes help quickly identify contents, and it is easer to write on a label than on a box. File folder labels on cords for electronics make setting back up a snap.

Other Helpful Supplies

- ◢ **Box cutters.** Get 3-4 box cutters with bright colored handles.
- ◢ **Furniture sliders.** These go under heavy furniture or appliances and allow things to be pushed across the floor easily.
- ◢ **Garbage bags.** It's helpful to have white and black, heavy-duty trash bags. Use one color for bulky things you can stuff (towels, stuffed animals, comforters and pillows.) Use the other color for trash.
- ◢ **Low tack tape.** Also called blue painter's tape, this is useful for keeping things together or closed where you don't want sticky residue.
- ◢ **Plastic zip storage bags.** Storage bags in pint and gallon sizes, for containing hardware for furniture you've taken apart and other loose, small objects.
- ◢ **Sharpie pens.** Sharpies or any type of permanent marker with a thick felt tip so you can read labels at a distance. Markers disappear like box cutters and tape so buy several.
- ◢ **Swiffer dust cloths.** If it's dusty or dirty, clean it before you pack it.
- ◢ **Tape measure.** Measuring first saves you time when you are trying to figure out where to fit something.
- ◢ **Tool apron.** Simple, inexpensive canvas pocket waist apron to keep markers, labels, tape, tape measure and box cutter handy.
- ◢ **Tool kit.** A basic tool kit and portable drill are useful for taking down shelving, lighting and other things you've installed but want to keep.
- ◢ **Twist or zip ties.** Great to keep extension cords and power strips held together.

General Packing Tips

Do Ahead

- Obtain good quality moving boxes, packing tape and plenty of packing paper.
- Have all supplies on hand before you start. See *Your Packing Supply Kit* (p. 61).
- Do research ahead of time on how to pack items that need special attention.
- Discuss with your movers ahead of moving day how you need to prep things that don't fit into boxes like computers, TVs (especially plasma TVs), other electronics, large tool boxes, delicate furniture and the like.

Packing

- The reason professional movers use clean newsprint (packing paper) for dishes, glassware, art, etc. is because it keeps everything clean. To save money you can use newspaper to fill in the rest of the box. You'll need a lot of it.
- Place heavier items in the bottom of a box.
- **Don't overload boxes.** The larger the box the lighter the contents should be.
- Have everything packed before moving day.
- Use as many same size boxes as possible. (This saves space in the moving van and allows your movers to load more quickly and efficiently.)
- Designate an area to stack packed boxes.
- Use mover's stretch wrap to secure drawers, lids, and other things that open.

Labeling

- Label boxes on the top, short side and long side to help you quickly identify what's in the box. See *Labeling Tips* (p. 63) for more helpful suggestions.
- Indicate in large letters in which room the box should be placed *in your new home*. This will save you a significant amount of time (and your back) when you begin unpacking.

The most common reason things break during a move is because of shifting. That's why professional packers use multiple layers of paper and tightly pack each box. Wadded paper eliminates air pockets between items and provides padding so nothing touches the sides, top or bottom of the box.

Labeling Tips

WE TAKE SPECIAL CARE WHEN LABELING CLIENT'S BOXES. They really appreciate it and comment on how helpful it is when unpacking. Properly labeled boxes make unpacking a pleasure because you can put your hands on almost anything you need immediately and push to the back the boxes you can deal with later.

Moving companies label boxes with general descriptions like "Kitchen – Dishes." However that doesn't tell you if it has your everyday set or the odd pieces you had in the back of the cupboard. If you are packing yourself follow our tips. They only take a few seconds and will save you time unpacking.

Labeling Tips

1. Use white large mailing labels, at least the 3"x4" size. We prefer these labels to the ones pre-stamped on the box. White labels stand out from a distance so they are easy to read.
2. Use a thick permanent marker (like a Sharpie).
3. In ALL CAPS write the name of the room where the box should go.
4. Draw a line under it.
5. Identify specific contents
6. Write other directions on the box itself (FRAGILE, THIS SIDE UP, etc.)

<u>**KITCHEN**</u>	<u>**GARAGE**</u>
Everyday glasses Measuring cups Salad bowls	Extension cords Rags Trash bags

7. Write other directions on the box itself.
8. Make 3 copies of each label.
9. Place labels on **3 sides** of box—the top, one short side and one long side. This way no matter how the box is stacked you can easily tell what is in it.

This may sound time consuming. We promise, it's worth it!

Packing Dishes & China

For crystal, china, dishware and stemware we recommend using "dish and glass pack" boxes. These boxes have double-sided walls for added strength and protection. Glass pack boxes have dividers that offer even more protection for fine crystal and stemware.

Plates and Flat China

1. Line the bottom of the carton with crumpled newsprint (4-8 sheets depending on size of box) or piece of bubble wrap to create a cushion.
2. With clean newsprint paper stacked neatly in place on a work surface, center one plate on the paper. Grasp a corner of the top piece of newsprint and fold it over the plate so the plate is completely covered. Place a second plate on top and pull a different corner of newsprint over the second plate. Stack a third plate and fold the remaining two corners over the plate.
3. Re-wrap the entire bundle of plates with two layers of newsprint, folding all four corners onto the top plate. Seal the bundle with packing tape.
4. Place the bundle of dishware in a medium-size box so that the plates are **standing on edge.**
5. As you fill the box, separate each level of plates with a thick layer of wadded paper or bubble wrap.

Crystal Glassware

1. Use special glass boxes with dividers. Delicate glassware and stemware should be placed in the dividers **rim side up**.
2. Lay the glass at a 45-degree angle on the corner of clean newsprint paper and roll it one or two full rotations (depending on size); pull sides of the newsprint paper up and over the rim, filling the bowl of the glass. Continue rolling to the far corner. Especially fragile items should be packed in a separate carton and then packed in a larger carton surrounded by cushioning.

Everyday Glassware and Mugs

You can use special glass boxes for your everyday glassware, or you can simply wrap each glass with two layers of newsprint, tucking the ends into the glass. Pad the bottom of the box and lay a single layer of glasses/mugs on the padding. Fill the spaces in each layer with newsprint. Separate each level with newsprint or bubble wrap.

If you wrap more than one item in a bundle, like a lid with a cookie jar or several small items together, make sure you mark the bundle with the number of items inside. It's very easy for something to get broken or tossed out when you are unpacking unless you're aware the bundle contains more than one item.

Packing Computers

Computers
1. Back up your files.
2. Remove CDs and DVDs from your computer.
3. Use file labels to tag each cord. Identify where it comes out of the computer and where and what it plugs into at the other end. Don't disconnect the plugs yet.
4. Photograph the back of your computer tower.
5. Unplug cords. Use twist ties to keep cords contained and together.
6. If you have original boxes and packaging materials (including Styrofoam) repack the equipment into those boxes.

Peripherals (printers, scanners, external hard drives, etc.)
1. Remove ink or toner cartridges and place in zip bags.
2. For printers, secure the print head.
3. For scanners or copiers, use low tack tape like blue painter's tape to hold down copier or scanner tops.
4. Secure cords and pack in original boxes if available.

If You Do Not Have Original Packaging
1. Select box 3"-4" larger on all sides than electronic equipment. Lay cushion of tightly wadded paper, solid Styrofoam or packing material on bottom. **DO NOT** use packing peanuts. They generate static electricity and can damage your electronic equipment.
2. For monitors and screens, cushion corners with bubble wrap, then wrap several times around with movers stretch wrap to protect screen.
3. Tightly tuck packing materials around all sides and top of computer. Tuck in cords so everything is in the same box.
4. Keep monitors in an upright position.
5. Label box. Mark FRAGILE and use arrow to indicate THIS SIDE UP.

Packing Large Screen Televisions and Electronics

Large Screen TVs (Plasma or LCD)

1. Check your television documentation for moving instructions.
2. If you are hiring movers, get their specific instructions. This is one item you may be better off hiring them to take care of for you.
3. Many warranties require that you use a qualified third-party service to pack your television even if you have the original packaging.
4. Crating may be recommended.

Do-It-Yourself Packing

1. Be aware of voiding your warranty. Even slight juggling of these televisions can break light projection bulbs, which are expensive to replace. You are fully responsible for damage.
2. Use file labels to tag each cord. Identify where it comes out of the television and where it plugs into other electronic devices. Do not disconnect the plugs yet.
3. Photograph the back of your television and associated electronics. Then disconnect plugs. (Don't assume you'll remember where everything goes.)
4. Gather all cords and power strip. Group together and pack the cords with one of the smaller electronic pieces, like a DVD player. Write "Cords for Television" on your box label so you can find them quickly when you go to set up your TV.
5. Plasma and LCD screens should never be laid screen side down. The weight can damage the screen. Keep the screen vertical and if you do lay it down keep it screen side up.
6. Lay a padded blanket over the screen and wrap many times around with movers shrink wrap or packing tape.
7. Move carefully into vehicle. Keep all sharp or blunt objects away from the screen and maintain the vertical position.
8. Plan ahead for cable wiring and television position in your new home so your TV can be moved as little as possible.

Hard to Pack Items

THERE ARE ALWAYS THINGS that are challenging to pack. Here we list some of the items commonly found in most homes. As in all packing, the principles are the same. Provide sufficient cushioning and padding so your items can't shift during moving. To save time, be sure to have all your supplies on hand before you start.

Small, Fragile Items

Wrapping fragile items is time consuming. If you are packing vases, bowls or other vessels, start by tucking clean tissue paper into open cavities.

1. Wrap generously with bubble wrap. For fine, delicate items use small sized bubble wrap. Cut thin strips and wrap several times around handles and other protruding pieces, Then wrap the entire object with bubble wrap and tape so there are no loose ends.
2. For very valuable items you can wrap again with custom cut lengths of cardboard.
3. Place in boxes with plenty of crumpled paper or foam packing peanuts to fill all air space. There should be 3-4" of cushioning on all sides of the box and nothing should touch the sides of the box.

Artwork

Wrap art in clean newsprint. Do not bring plastic wrap into contact with art surfaces. Bubble wrap can be used to protect the edges of frames after paper wrapping. You can purchase special art boxes or cut a box to custom fit your piece.

Framed Photographs

Many people have photographs in inexpensive frames. Wrap each photo frame in a few sheets of clean newsprint. Stack in boxes vertically in groups of two with glass sides facing each other.

Lamps

Remove harps and other hardware and light bulbs. Pack bases in boxes or wrap with blankets. Put finials, screws or other hardware in a small zip bag and tape it to the inside of the box.

Lampshades are easily damaged. Select a box slightly larger than the lampshade. Place crumpled paper in the bottom of the box. Set in the lampshade and gently stuff clean packing paper around the sides and in the center of the shade. Be sure and mark the box FRAGILE. To quickly reassemble your lamps, label both the lamp base box and shade box with the same name (i.e., Lamp – master bedside table).

Crating

Crates are usually built for valuable furniture and art. If you have pieces that need crating it is best to hire a professional.

Save on Full Service Moves

UNLESS YOU HAVE A PAID FOR, TOP-OF-THE-LINE CORPORATE RELOCATION PACKAGE, you may have sticker shock when you get bids on your full service move. They are expensive, but having all the backbreaking work done for you, not to mention the time you will save, make the cost worth it for many people. If you have decided to hire full service movers, below are ways to get the best deal possible.

Money-Saving Tips

◢ Ask for discounts. Most moving company charges are based on fees from *Tariff 400*, published by the American Moving and Storage Association. They determine the highest price movers can charge based on weight and distance. Most movers discount from this fee at least 40%. Ask your mover how much they discount from the *Tariff 400* and negotiate from there.

◢ Try to avoid moving during June and July. Since most families move then, that is the moving "high season" and charges are higher.

◢ Be flexible on the day and time of move. If you can work with your mover's timeframe, it can save you money. The beginning and end of the month are the most expensive.

◢ Read the chapter *organizing for Your Move* and get to work   Moving fewer things results in instant cost savings.

◢ Be clear on all additional charges for large/fragile items. Pianos, pool tables and large appliances will have additional charges associated with them. Specialty movers may offer a better price on those items.

◢ Be prepared on moving day. If you are packing yourself, be finished the night before. If there are movers standing around waiting for you to pack a box, you are going to be charged extra.

◢ Make sure your new home will be ready to move in to. If your belongings are on the truck and you can't move into your new home, everything is put in storage and you will be charged extra.

◢ Make sure you have funds available to pay the movers immediately at your new home. They will require that you pay in full. Otherwise, your belongings will be put into their storage facility and you will be charged extra for storage fees.

Hazardous or Prohibited Items

YOUR FULL-SERVICE MOVING COMPANY cannot transport items that are on their hazardous materials list, and some of those items you might want to consider not moving at all. While you should ask your mover for their specific list, use these guidelines:

Hazardous Items

- Explosives
- Loaded guns
- Flammable liquids and solids
- Poisons
- Corrosive and radioactive materials
- Oxidizers
- Compressed gases

There are many common household items included in these categories. These items should not be packed and put in a moving van. If you want to bring these things with you, take them in your car. Packing these items for loading on a moving van will limit your mover's liability if something is damaged.

Common Household Items Considered Hazardous for a Move

- Nail polish remover
- Aerosol cans
- Propane cylinders
- Fire extinguishers
- Batteries
- Matches
- Opened bottles of wine or alcohol
- Champagne
- Ammonia, bleach and vinegar
- Dishwashing liquid and laundry detergent
- Pesticides, weed killers and fertilizers
- Motor oil
- Paints and paint thinners

If you need to dispose of any of these hazardous products, contact your local municipality or trash service. Many cities have hazardous waste disposal drop off sites that accept these products.

Be Prepared for Moving Day

CONGRATULATIONS! MOVING DAY HAS ARRIVED. Everything is packed, and you're ready to go. Even with good planning, moving day is going to be a chaotic experience. Whether you have hired movers or have your best friends helping you, the tips below will minimize the chaos and make the process easier.

Supplies to Have On Hand
- Tool kit with several box cutters.
- Furniture sliders.
- A dolly is handy to move stacks of boxes and heavy items.
- "S" hooks are great to temporarily shorten chandelier chains so heads are safe.
- See *Organizing Supplies for Settling In* (p. 75) for a complete list of everything we like to have on hand for settling in.

Prepare Your New Home
- Clear the driveway or on-street parking for the moving van.
- Make a sign for the door of each room, labeling it with the identification name on the packing boxes.
- If you have a furniture placement plan, put it in a convenient place so movers can refer to it.
- Have refreshments on hand—water and sodas are greatly appreciated.
- A plan to keep pets and children out of the way and safe is important.
- As soon as they arrive, take the movers on a tour of the home.
- Protect your floors.

Extras Tips for Assisting Your Professional Movers
- Have your inventory list in hand. Assign a person to stand at the door and check off every item. Make notes of anything that is damaged.
- Offer to provide lunch for your movers. (Remember, if they leave for lunch, they take all your belongings with them for a ride around town.)
- The driver will ask you to sign each page of the inventory list. It is good practice to write "subject to inspection" in case something is broken and you need to submit a claim.

Tipping Movers
Like anyone in a service industry, moving crews appreciate tips. For a full day's move we suggest $20 per person. If someone goes out of the way for you or if your move is particularly challenging (steep driveway, many stairs, etc.) consider up to $50 per person. Be sure to have cash on hand for tips.

Settling In

Making Your New Home "Yours"

After the Dust Settles

After The Movers Depart — First Things First

YOU AND YOUR BELONGINGS ARE NOW AGAIN IN THE SAME PLACE—YOUR NEW HOME. The movers have done their job and the empty truck has driven away. However, instead of being ready to tackle the piles of boxes in every room, you are probably exhausted. The tips below will help make the rest of the day as productive as possible.

Have a plan for the next few days for the kids and pets. Moving is traumatic for them and they will need supervision to make sure they adjust to their new surroundings.

Unpacking Tips for Moving Day

- ◢ Assemble beds.
- ◢ Locate and unpack each room's "open first" box.
- ◢ Your kitchen box should contain your tool kit.
- ◢ If you have a landline, connect it. If you have a new number, post it in an obvious place.
- ◢ Make sure every room has light. Check overhead lights for working bulbs and unpack lamps for rooms with inadequate overhead lighting.
- ◢ Check your appliances. You want the washer, dryer, refrigerator and ice maker to be up and running.
- ◢ Designate the empty box and packing material area.
- ◢ Make sure each bathroom has toilet paper, soap and a towel.
- ◢ Make a quick run to the store for the basics—milk, bread, paper towels, etc.
- ◢ Get the Internet connection, cable and at least one TV up and running (especially for the kids.)
- ◢ Order out or escape the boxes and go out for dinner. It's hard washing dishes when you haven't unpacked the dish soap.

Settling In

IT'S TIME TO MAKE YOU NEW HOUSE A HOME. Most of our clients are so caught up in the packing and moving process they forget unpacking is an equally big job. Here's what we've learned about getting settled in:

Make a Plan

▲ **Create a mini command post.** This is the place (usually the kitchen) where you keep your notepad, phone, phone book, business cards, this workbook, and the toolbox.

▲ **Prioritize unpacking tasks.** This is dependent on your family situation. If you cook for five every day, get the kitchen done. If you work from home, set up the study. For more information on unpacking see the specific articles in this chapter.

▲ **Purchase organizing supplies.** From closet systems to drawer dividers, purchasing organizing supplies for your new home is necessary. Check out our article *Organizing Supplies for Settling In* (p. 75) to create your list.

▲ **Break tasks into smaller, doable chunks.** Allot a certain period of time, say 2-3 hours, for unpacking an area. Then take a break.

▲ **Get packing materials out.** Break down boxes and remove packing paper as you go. See *Packing Materials Disposal* (p.83) for ideas on disposing of your packing materials.

▲ **Test your appliances.** We've been on several jobs where dishwashers and washing machines flooded. This happens when appliances are hooked up improperly. Make sure they work correctly before walking away.

▲ **Schedule cable/Internet and other services ASAP.** People feel unsettled until their services are hooked up. If possible, schedule these in advance so your service will be available quickly.

Take Care of Yourself and Your Family

▲ **Routines.** Establish normal routines as quickly as possible. If you exercise every morning do that. Get the kids going, the pets fed on their normal schedule. Routines relieve stress.

▲ **Get out and explore.** Break up the unpacking day with a trip to the grocery store, your favorite big box store, the gas station, the park. It's reassuring to know you can find the services you need.

▲ **Hire help.** Sometimes there is one room or task you just can't seem to face. It may be setting up your garage, or home office, getting all your electronics set up or hanging the pictures. Consider hiring someone to help you tackle the task. With help, many of these jobs can be completed in a couple hours.

Organizing Supplies for Settling In

UPACKING AND SETTLING IN QUICKLY STALLS if you need to keep running to the store to get organizing supplies. In addition to large organizing systems for closets and garages, there are many smaller items that help you organize your new home. There are certain things everyone needs to set up a new home. Here is our basic supply list for settling in. Buy more than you think you'll need, get different styles. Use what works and return the rest. This method makes the most of your limited time.

Organizing Supplies for All Rooms

Drawer dividers
Clear bins, baskets
Various sized boxes/storage containers
Shelf dividers
Expandable shelving
Label maker or Sharpie pens
Cleaning products
Cleaning caddy
Picture hanging supplies
3M Command hooks and strips
Trash cans
Contact paper
Non-skid drawer mats

Kitchen Organizing Supplies

Silverware organizer
Drawer dividers
Paper towel holder
Grocery bag holder
Pot lid organizer
Dish rack
Towel holder
Spice storage
Knife storage

Garage Organizing Supplies

Storage shelves
Tool racks/organizers
Hooks (variety of sizes)
Bike rack
Sports equipment organizer

Closet Organizing Supplies

Closet organizing systems
Drawer dividers (socks, underwear)
Accessory organizer (jewelry, belts)
Hooks
Hangers (all matching, no wire)
Shoe racks

Office Organizing Supplies

File organizers
Cable ties
Book/storage shelves

Prioritize Unpacking Tasks

YOU'VE SET UP BEDS AND A BASIC KITCHEN. In our experience people flit from room to room, pull a few things out of boxes and then get distracted to another room. No wonder everything feels like chaos. Make the most of your time by prioritizing unpacking decisions based on your lifestyle.

Unpack Essentials
Make a list of your family priorities. For example, if you work outside the home and need specific clothes, immediately setting up your closet is important. Work at home? Unpack your office essentials and get your computer, phone and network set up. Got kids? Unpacking their bedrooms, setting up a playroom, TV or computer is high on your list. If you followed the suggestions from *Labeling Tips* (p. 63) it will be easy to find what you need.

Make Time for Unpacking the Rest
To stay on track and get your home totally unpacked, schedule unpacking sessions like you would a dinner out or a kid's play date. Get the family involved to get the job done quickly.

Have a Variety of Storage Containers On Hand.
A big reason people get stuck when they start unpacking is they don't have the right organizing tools on hand. See our list of commonly needed items in *Organizing Supplies for Settling In* (p. 75).

Unpack Systematically
Tackle one room at a time. You will accomplish more in less time. Flatten and neatly stack unpacked boxes as you go. The faster boxes are torn down and things put away the sooner you will feel at home.

For great ideas on setting up specific rooms see *Setting Up Your Kitchen* (p. 78), *Closets That Work* (p. 79), *Create a Functional Home Office* (p. 80), *and The Well-Organized Garage* (p. 81).

Hire Help
Many people waste time and become frustrated trying to set up their computers, wireless networks and televisions. Save your sanity, hire a professional. Test everything yourself before your service person leaves.

Effective Organizing Solutions

THERE ARE BASIC STORAGE PRINCIPLES that work for any room in the house. Keep these in mind as you unpack your home.

General Rules

- ◢ Place the things you use often between knee and shoulder level.
- ◢ Invest in a label maker. They aren't expensive, and well-labeled containers look great.
- ◢ Keep things together that belong together.
- ◢ Everything becomes disorganized over time. Once a year do a thorough cleaning and straightening to get everything back into shape.

Closet/Garage Organizing Systems

- ◢ Don't think closet or garage organizing systems are out of your price range. An inexpensive wire mesh system you install yourself is as useful as a custom, professionally installed system costing thousands more.
- ◢ Look for flexibility. A closet system with adjustable shelves is worth the extra cost. Also look for systems that have accessories, like drawers and shelves that can be purchased separately.
- ◢ There are a variety of specialty products designed to store purses, hats, ties, scarves, and shoes. Check them out.
- ◢ If you are installing an your system make sure to have the tools and hardware to complete the job.
- ◢ If you move frequently and want to take a closet or garage organizing system with you, make sure the system you purchase can be easily disassembled.

Decorative Storage

- ◢ Baskets, tin bins, hatboxes and pretty boxes can all be used to keep your things organized and your room beautiful as well.
- ◢ Use magazine holders to keep magazines and papers out of sight.

Storage Containers

- ◢ Square shapes are more space efficient than round.
- ◢ Clear containers allow you to see the contents.
- ◢ Label containers and shelves.
- ◢ Find storage containers with lids that stack well.

Organizers

- ◢ Use drawer organizers for easy, efficient access.
- ◢ Don't forget the back of the door. Use a back-of-the-door organizer.

Setting Up Your Kitchen

IT PAYS TO THINK THROUGH where you want everything to go in your kitchen before unpacking anything.

- Compare your old and new kitchens. Is there more or less cupboard, pantry and storage space?
- Make a list of what you didn't like about your old kitchen so you can make those changes in your new one.
- Plan out where you want everything to go. Don't let your friends unpack your kitchen. It might be years before you find your favorite vegetable peeler.

Basic Design Considerations

- Plan around the things you use everyday—glassware, silverware, dishes, basic pots and pans. Consider the location of your dishwasher. You don't want to climb over the open door when unloading it.
- Know the widths of your drawers. Will your current utensil dividers fit? Will you need more or different sizes?
- Measure your tallest everyday glasses and stacks of plates. Adjust shelves accordingly.
- Group like with like. For the kitchen, this means create a prep area, baking center, cleaning center, cooking center. Everything you need for that particular function should be in easy reach.
- Make use of under cabinet and wall space. Metal strips can hold knives, utensils and spice containers.
- Designate a catch-all (junk) drawer. Organize it with drawer dividers.

Things to Consider

- Create a snack area in a drawer, shelf or cupboard. If you have kids make sure it is at a level they can reach.
- If your cabinets are a mess and you need to be a gymnast to get your pots and pans out, install pullout shelves or drawers for easy access to lower cabinets.
- Square containers stack easily and make the most efficient use of space.
- Kitchen items you use a couple times a year don't have to be in the kitchen.
- Don't cook in the dark. Under counter fluorescent or halogen lighting illuminates your countertops.
- There are many options for trash and recycling containers. For new ideas, visit your local home improvement center.

Closets That Work

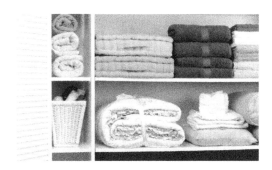

WELL-ORGANIZED CLOSETS ARE A JOY. They save you time and frustration.

Basic Principles for Organizing Any Closet

- Think in zones: Every clothes closet needs a shoe, shirt, pants, dress, and accessories zone. Likewise a linen closet needs areas for bedding, towels, toiletries and medicine.
- Use every inch of space. There are great closet shelving systems in every price range. Adjustable shelves will give you the most flexibility.
- Fold efficiently. The Real Simple website has some great tutorials at *realsimple.com*. (Type "How to Fold Anything" in the search box.)

Clothes Closets

- Single rods are for dresses and pants hung by the cuffs. Use double rods for shirts, jackets and pants hung over hangers.
- Hanging rods should be 12" away from the back wall of the closet. Shelving for clothing should be shallow, no more than 14".
- Baskets or clear bins are perfect for holding underwear and socks if you do not have enough drawers.
- Matching hangers instantly make a closet look organized.
- If you need to store things on the floor put them in containers, bins, or shelves.

Linens

- Group bedding and towels by room or size.
- A good rule of thumb is two sets of sheets for each bed you have.
- A nifty trick for keeping sheet sets together is to place the bottom and top sheets inside a matching pillowcase.
- Discard mismatched sheets and towels.
- Bulky, lightweight and less frequently used items go on the top shelf.
- Linens take on a musty smell when they are packed too tightly.
- Wire shelf dividers keep stacks of sheets and towels upright.

Medicine Cabinets

- Use clear bins for grouping your medicines. Busy families can subdivide medicine and first aid items into smaller bins. Make it easy to find something fast by grouping pain relievers, cough & cold, and first aid separately.
- For medicine cabinets use small containers to keep items together like Q-tips, cotton balls, hair clips.
- Medicine should not be stored in bathroom cabinets. Store in a nearby closet.

Create a Functional Home Office

DEPENDING ON YOUR LIFESTYLE AND THE SIZE OF YOUR HOME, a home office can be a dedicated room, a corner of the family room or a nook in the kitchen. However big or small it is make your home office as functional as possible.

Frequently a home office serves more than one purpose. It could be a place where both husband and wife work, a space where kids play while mom or dad works, or an all-purpose room where hobbies are nurtured.

The article *Your Organizational Style* (p. 25) will get you started on new ways to arrange your office, and *Sorting Your Paper Clutter* (p. 31) with organizing your papers.

Unpacking

- Start by unpacking your office essentials. Make it functional first, especially in small spaces, before you start adding decorative touches.
- Don't put things in the office area if they don't belong there. Keep a box handy for items you unpack that belong somewhere else.

Sharing Space

- If you can, create a separate work area for each person, or at least a separate area for each person's personal items. This can reduce shared space frustrations.
- A large horizontal surface in an office is versatile. If space is tight and a worktable is not practical, we recommend a folding sewing/craft/cutting table. They can be purchased for around $100 and fold down to store.
- If kids will be sharing the office area, create easily accessible storage for toys and art supplies.
- Hobbies like scrapbooking and activities like gift wrapping are often done, or at least stored, in the home office. Investigate storage containers made specifically for those activities to maximize storage.

Reducing Clutter

- Use cable ties to keep cables under control.
- When the time comes for a new printer consider a wireless all-in-one machine that combines the printer, scanner, fax machine and copier into one unit.
- Make sure everything has an identified place to be in the office. If you know where everything goes, it will be easier to keep the office neat.

The Well-Organized Garage

A **WELL-ORGANIZED GARAGE** is one of the most useful areas in a home. Here are some tips to get your garage to work for you.

Storage Ideas

- ◢ Wall mounted shelves keep things off the floor. Use brackets and hooks for gardening tools.
- ◢ Floor to ceiling storage is practical in the garage. Long-term storage can go high, while frequently used things can be at eye level.
- ◢ Consider cabinets with doors to keep things clean, dust free, and give your garage an uncluttered look. Before you purchase cabinets, make sure the shelves are deep enough to hold your storage containers.
- ◢ If storage is tight, don't forget the ceiling. Shelving is available that mounts to the ceiling or hangs from exposed beams. It's a great place for storing seasonal decorations, luggage, and electronics boxes.
- ◢ Many families use a part of the garage as a pantry for items bought in bulk. Keep these items close to the door to the house for easy accessibility.

Tools, Gardening Supplies and Sporting Goods

- ◢ Create separate areas for categories of things (tools, sporting goods etc.) so they will be easy to find and replace.
- ◢ If you have lots of sporting goods, consider special units made for storing balls, bats, hockey sticks, etc.
- ◢ A bike rack keeps bikes upright and off the floor. Hanging the bikes on the wall or from the ceiling by the front wheel are other options.
- ◢ A pegboard installed above a workbench keeps your tools visible and easy to find. Draw an outline around each tool to keep them tidy and so you can see at a glance if something is missing.
- ◢ Tools sometimes come in storage cases that are hard to keep closed. Use plastic storage containers (like Rubbermaid Roughnecks) to store a drill with all bits, a saw with all blades, a sander with all sandpaper, etc. Label each container.

Other Suggestions

- ◢ To discourage rodents and pests, store pet food stored in a container with a tight seal.
- ◢ If you have dangerous chemicals or pesticides make sure they are out of the reach of children or in a locked cabinet.
- ◢ Don't store anything that could be adversely affected by temperature and humidity fluctuations in the garage. Antiques, fabric and photos can be damaged.

Hang Pictures Like the Pros

PICTURES ON THE WALLS INSTANTLY MAKE A HOUSE FEEL LIKE A HOME. Hanging pictures is time consuming so if you have a lot of things to hang give yourself enough time. These are our favorite picture hanging techniques.

General Rules

◢ Pictures should be hung at eye level, 60" from the floor to the center of the picture.

◢ One small picture on a large wall or a huge picture on a small wall looks unbalanced. On large walls use a collection of small frames, add a mirror, or add a shelf for decorative items.

◢ Collections of pictures make interesting focal points. Try grouping four same-size pictures or a grouping of a large picture flanked by two smaller pictures.

◢ Use similar frames (silver or black frames with different patterning) with white mats to make your family photos look professional.

◢ For a more eclectic look, attach ribbon to pictures and use decorative picture nails or knobs for hanging.

◢ If you have more pictures than wall space, consider attaching a picture rail to the wall and have a rotating display of pictures.

◢ Don't hang pictures until you are happy with your furniture placement.

Tips

◢ Use picture hangers, not nails in the wall.

◢ Use two hangers for larger pictures to keep the picture level.

◢ Use a pencil (easy to erase) to mark where a picture should hang.

◢ Picture hanging is easier with someone to help you.

◢ With large, heavy pictures or mirrors screw picture hangers directly into a stud.

◢ To hang a collection of pictures, cut paper templates. Arrange them on the walls with painters tape.

◢ Don't trust your eyes. Use a level.

Measuring

To determine where the picture hanger should be nailed into the wall, use this two-step method.

1. Measure the picture from top to bottom and add half that number to 60". That is the measurement where the top of the picture should be.

2. Hold the hanging wire taut with your finger, like it is being hung on a hook. (If you are using two hooks, hold the wire taut with two fingers.) Measure the distance from the top of the picture to your finger. Subtract that number from the first number. That is where the part of the hanger that holds the wire should be on the wall.

Packing Materials Disposal

It's amazing how quickly boxes and paper accumulate as you unpack. Crumbled paper is bulky and soon you have so many boxes, it's hard to tell which ones are empty and which ones aren't. Packing materials from even a very small move can fill up a garage fast. Use these tips to keep things under control.

Strategies to Minimize the Attack of the Boxes

- Pick a holding area for all the boxes/paper. The garage is a good place.
- Break down boxes as you unpack.
- Unpack a couple medium to large size boxes and don't break them down. Use these to hold packing paper.
- Unpack wrapped items on a horizontal surface. Do a quick smoothing of paper and create a (somewhat neat) stack. When it gets too high put the paper into your reserved boxes.

Tips for Disposal of Packing Materials

Some people want to sell their packing boxes to recoup costs. Others are happy to have the boxes and paper out of their hair. Please don't send your boxes and paper to the trash. There are many creative ways to sell, recycle or reuse the materials.

- Ask your real estate agent if he/she (or someone in the office) has a client who needs packing materials.
- Ask your moving company representative if they take boxes.
- Post a listing on *craigslist.org*. Here's an example of how we would post on Craigslist: "FREE, 50 small-sized, broken-down packing boxes, 2 large boxes full of packing paper. These boxes fill the back of a mini-van. Must take everything. Call xxx-xxxx." Note that we say in the listing "must take everything" and we give an idea of the size of vehicle needed to haul the boxes away. You don't have time to deal with people only taking a few boxes at a time. The objective is to get them out.
- Take the boxes/paper to your local recycle center.
- If you purchased your boxes from U-Haul ask if they have a free box exchange.

Boxes Not Unpacked?

DO YOU HAVE UNPACKED BOXES WEEKS AFTER YOUR MOVE? We're not talking about things that are always in boxes, like seasonal decorations, but boxes full of things that really should be unpacked. We usually find those unpacked boxes are still there for one of three reasons.

- ▲ You don't have time to unpack anymore.
- ▲ You've run out of space and don't know where to put it.
- ▲ You haven't had a need for it.

Our first and foremost suggestion to solve this problem is to **hire a professional organizer** to get the job done quickly and painlessly. It is less expensive than you think, and they will be able to bring a wealth of knowledge and an unbiased eye to your home. If hiring someone is really out of your budget, try these ideas.

Don't Have Time?

Once essential boxes are unpacked and your daily routine is established, it's common to have a hard time getting back to unpacking boxes.

- ▲ Don't let the job overwhelm you. Break it into small chunks of time. Promise yourself to unpack one box per day until the job is done.
- ▲ Get family and friends to help.
- ▲ Use an event like a party or house guests to impose a deadline on yourself.

Don't Know Where to Put It?

Do you feel like you've simply run out of space, yet there are more boxes to be unpacked?

- ▲ Search out new solutions. *HGTV.com*, your local Target or Walmart, and home improvement stores have great solutions for storage and organizing dilemmas.
- ▲ Do you have a friend whose home always looks great? Friends are a great resource for seeing your home with "fresh eyes" and might be able to offer advice for revamping your storage spaces or moving things around to create more room for your belongings.
- ▲ Are you sure you really need it? You haven't used it in a while...

Haven't Had a Need for It?

In our experience, this situation almost always means you don't really need or want the things in the box (unless it's seasonal.) If you loved it or used it, you would have already unpacked it.

- ▲ Unpack the boxes and look at the contents again. Revisit our article *Letting Go Is Hard* (p. 22) and *Sorting Strategies* (p. 26)
- ▲ If you decide to keep things, incorporate them into your household right away.

Keeping Your New Home Clutter Free

HAVING THINGS IN ORDER is a way to make your life calmer and easier but it's not always an easy task. Maintaining a clutter free home requires dedication and a good plan.

Proven Strategies for Keeping Your House Clutter Free

- If you get it out, put it away. It's a deceptively easy rule that gets broken all the time.
- Make sure everything has a place in your home. Clutter escalates when things that don't have a specific place to live.
- Choose multi-tasking products. Alton Brown from The Food Network loves kitchen tool that do multiple jobs. We do too!
- Use the "one in, one out" rule. If you buy something new, something needs to be donated, sold or thrown away.
- Keep a box or bag for charity donations in an easily accessible place.
- Cull toys and kids clothes regularly. Back-to-school is a good time.
- Simplify—the less you have the easier it is to keep track of it all.
- Cut back on paper—switch to paperless billing. Cancel catalogs and receive e-newsletters for companies you like instead.
- Create a daily declutter routine. Set a timer for 10-15 minutes and pick one small area, say a drawer or one shelf, to clean out each day. That little bit of work can adds up to a neater house!
- One of our friends, a divorced, full-time working mother goes through a routine each evening she calls "putting the house to bed." She and her daughter do a 10-minute sweep through the house and return things to their proper place. This is a wonderful habit for kids to develop.
- If you need ideas on ways of selling or donating things you find you no longer need in your new home, look back at the chapter Donating and Selling.

Online Resources That Keep Us Motivated and Inspired

- *Unclutterer.com* (blog about getting and staying organized)
- *43Folders.com* (time and paper management)
- *Lifehacker.com* (technological tips to get things done)
- *Simplemoves.net* (strategies and products to simplify your move)

Checklists and Worksheets

Tasks to Complete

THIS CHECKLIST OF TASKS will help keep you on track as your move grows closer. Use it in tandem with *Notifications to Make (p. 92)* for a comprehensive list of things to do for your move.

The Big Decisions
- ☐ Interview and contract with a reputable real estate agent (you may need two agents, one to sell your home and one to act as your buyer's agent if you are moving to a new city).
- ☐ Choose a mortgage lender and request a pre-qualification letter.
- ☐ Decide how you will move. Do-it-yourself, full-service or something in-between.
- ☐ Take a household inventory, complete with pictures.
- ☐ If your move is work related check the IRS guidelines to determine if your move is tax deductible. See *Is Your Move Tax Deductible? (p. 4.)* If you qualify, keep all your moving receipts in one of the pockets of this workbook.

Selling Your Home
- ☐ Sort and declutter.
- ☐ Work with your real estate agent to get your home ready to show by scheduling needed repairs, cleaning thoroughly and sprucing up the yard.
- ☐ Stage your home to attract prospective buyers.
- ☐ When someone signs a contract to purchase your home, get a list from your real estate agent of all appointments and meetings you are required to attend.

Purchasing Your New Home
- ☐ Sign the real estate contract to purchase the home.
- ☐ Work with your buyer's agent to schedule all necessary appointments; inspections, appraisals, title insurance, etc.
- ☐ Complete your loan application.
- ☐ Schedule your closing date.
- ☐ After purchase, obtain homeowner's insurance on new home.

Getting Ready for the Move
- ☐ Plan a going away party.
- ☐ Give appropriate notice to landlord if you are a renter.
- ☐ Get bids from moving companies and schedule your move.
- ☐ Purchase your packing materials if you will be packing yourself.
- ☐ Create your furniture layout plan for your new home.
- ☐ Pre-measure furniture and appliances. Make sure they will fit through doors and hallways in your new home.
- ☐ Use the *Notifications to Make (p. 92)* checklist to start contacting all necessary agencies, businesses and personal friends about your move.

Tasks to Complete—continued

☐ Start planning meals around food already in your pantry or freezer to reduce what you will move or need to throw away.

☐ Continue decluttering and organizing.

☐ Clear your home of hazardous and hard-to-dispose items that cannot be moved.

☐ If you are packing yourself, start packing seldom used or out-of-season things.

☐ Plan and arrange for pet transfer.

☐ Change address on luggage tags.

☐ Transfer school records.

☐ Arrange for moving day baby or pet sitter.

☐ Sort personal papers. Separate documents that will travel with you and put them in a portable file box. A helpful list is *Things to Keep with You* (p. 54).

☐ Gather all instruction manuals, warranties and accessories for things that stay in the home. Put them in a box and label, "Do Not Move—For New Owners."

☐ Reconfirm moving dates with moving company. Verify method of payment (obtain cashiers check if necessary.)

☐ Finish packing, except for items you need up to moving day.

☐ Movers do not remove picture hooks or drapery hardware from walls. Do this yourself if needed.

☐ Pack your "Open Me First" boxes for each room.

☐ Make sure everything is packed the day before the movers arrive.

After the Move

☐ Arrange for cleaning of old home.

☐ Document items damaged in transit and submit to moving company.

☐ Get pet licensed in new location.

☐ Re-key all exterior doors and re-program garage door code.

☐ See *Packing Materials Disposal* (p 83) for ideas on getting boxes and paper out of your house.

Documents to Keep

AS YOU GO THROUGH YOUR FILING SYSTEM AND PERSONAL DOCUMENTS BEFORE YOU MOVE, you will have questions about what to keep and what to shred or throw away. Below is a general list of documents you should keep and move to your new home. Since rules change from year to year, if you are uncertain or hesitant to throw documents away, it's a good idea to check with your tax accountant or the IRS at *irs.gov/taxtopics/tc305.html*.

Keep for Four Years After Last Transaction or Filing
- ☐ Tax returns and all backup documentation
- ☐ Records associated with the sale/purchase of a property, including home improvement receipts
- ☐ Investment records
- ☐ Retirement plan records

Keep with Tax Return if Needed as Supporting Documentation
- ☐ Bank statements
- ☐ Credit card statements
- ☐ Household receipts
- ☐ Mortgage statements
- ☐ Relocation expense receipts
- ☐ Homeowner's final settlement statement (in escrow paperwork)

Keep Current
- ☐ Will and living trust
- ☐ Insurance policies, including home/renter, auto, life, health
- ☐ Stock certificates and savings bonds
- ☐ Medical/dental records
- ☐ Motor vehicle titles
- ☐ Car licensing documents
- ☐ Record of household inventory
- ☐ Appraisal documents

Keep Forever
- ☐ Passports
- ☐ Birth, marriage and death certificates
- ☐ Adoption records
- ☐ Military records
- ☐ Social security cards

ıications to Make

USE ᴛʜɪꜱ ᴏꜰ **Nᴏᴛɪꜰɪᴄᴀᴛɪᴏɴꜱ** to make sure you've contacted all the appropriate agencies, businesses and personal connections about your move.

Government
- [x] Post Office
  - o Change of address
  - o ~~Cancel current~~ PO box and order one at your new location
- [ ] IRS
- [ ] Social Security Administration
- [ ] State and Local Tax Offices
- [ ] Motor Vehicle Registration
- [ ] Voter Registration
- [ ] Driver's License

Financial
- [ ] ~~Accountant~~
- [ ] Bank Accounts
  - o Don't forget your direct deposits and automatic withdrawals if you are closing your current bank account
  - o If you aren't changing banks you will still need new checks with your new address
  - o If you have a safe deposit box, plan how to transport the contents to your new bank
- [ ] Credit Card Accounts
  - o Cancel cards at local stores that will not be in your new location
- [ ] Loan Accounts   Ca
  - o Make sure the old mortgage company (from the home you are selling) has your new address
- [x] Investment Accounts E-mailed Steve (letter
- [ ] ~~Airline Mileage Accounts~~
- [ ] ~~Workplace~~

Subscriptions
- [ ] ~~Magazines~~
- [ ] ~~Newspapers~~
- [ ] ~~Newsletters~~
- [ ] ~~Book/CD Clubs~~
- [ ] ~~Catalogs~~

Notifications to Make—continued

Medical

If you are moving away from your city and will not be able to keep the same medical professionals, check with each before you leave to determine their recommended way of transferring medical records to your new providers.

- ☐ Doctors
- ☐ Hospitals
- ☐ Dentists
- ☐ Pharmacies
  - o Get all prescriptions filled before the move
- ☑ Health Insurance Providers
  - o Get a list of approved providers in your new location to identify possible new doctors

Professionals

- ☐ Lawyer
- ☐ Veterinarian
- ☐ Babysitter
- ☐ Auto/Car/Home Insurance Providers
  - o Go over your coverage with your agent to understand your coverage during the move
  - o Don't cancel your old homeowners coverage until your new coverage is in effect and you have inspected your belongings for damage during the move
  - o Now is a great time to look at all your policies for gaps or over- coverage and get new quotes
  - o Put new car insurance ID cards in each car

Businesses

- ☐ House Cleaners
- ☐ Lawn Maintenance
- ☐ Dry Cleaners
  - o Don't forget to pick up any remaining clothes!
- ☐ Public Library
  - o Return all books before you move
- ☐ Dairy Delivery
- ☐ Exterminator
- ☐ Auto Mechanic
  - o If moving cross country, schedule a car check before the drive
- ☐ Movie Rental
  - o Return all movies and/or video games

Notifications to Make—continued

Associations
- ☐ Schools
    - o Check procedure for getting school records transferred
    - o Make a list of other records the new school will require (vaccinations, school physical, birth certificate) and keep those together and handy
- ☐ Daycare Facilities
- ☐ Church
- ☐ Library
- ☐ Gym
- ☐ Sports Clubs

Social
- ☐ Family
- ☐ Friends
- ☐ Colleagues

Utilities
- ☑ Electric
- ☐ Gas
- ☐ Cable
    - o Return cable boxes and remotes if they were a part of your service
- ☐ Internet
    - o Return modem if a part of your service
- ☐ Phone
- ☐ Cell phone Provider
- ☐ Garbage
- ☐ Water/Sewer
- ☐ Security System

Address Change Notifications

Business/Person_____

Phone_____Notice Date_____

Notes_____

Business/Person_____

Phone_____Notice Date_____

Notes_____

Business/Person_____

Phone_____Notice Date_____

Notes_____

Business/Person_____

Phone_____Notice Date_____

Notes_____

Business/Person_____

Phone_____Notice Date_____

Notes_____

Service Cancellations

Type of Service_____

Phone_____Notice Date_____

Time and Day of Last Service_____

Notes_____

Type of Service_____

Phone_____Notice Date_____

Time and Day of Last Service_____

Notes_____

Type of Service_____

Phone_____Notice Date_____

Time and Day of Last Service_____

Notes_____

Type of Service_____

Phone_____Notice Date_____

Time and Day of Last Service_____

Notes_____

New Services

THIS WORKSHEET CAN HELP YOU KEEP TRACK OF THE NEW SERVICES YOU ORDER FOR YOUR NEW HOME.

Type of Service____

Phone________________________ Start Date____________________

Service Time and Day____________________________________

Notes____

Type of Service____

Phone________________________ Start Date____________________

Service Time and Day____________________________________

Notes____

Type of Service____

Phone________________________ Start Date____________________

Service Time and Day____________________________________

Notes____

Type of Service____

Phone________________________ Start Date____________________

Service Time and Day____________________________________

Notes____

Service Transfers

IF YOUR MOVE IS LOCAL, THERE MAY BE SERVICES THAT SIMPLY NEED TO BE TRANSFERRED FROM ONE ADDRESS TO ANOTHER.

Type of Service_____

Phone_____Notice Date_____

Last Service at Old Home_____First Service at New Home_____

Notes_____

Type of Service_____

Phone_____Notice Date_____

Last Service at Old Home_____First Service at New Home_____

Notes_____

Type of Service_____

Phone_____Notice Date_____

Last Service at Old Home_____First Service at New Home_____

Notes_____

Type of Service_____

Phone_____Notice Date_____

Last Service at Old Home_____First Service at New Home_____

Notes_____

Index

Index - Continued

Notes

Need more copies?

Order Online:
www.organizepackmove.com

Email:
info@simplemoves.net

Call or Fax:
p. 303.552.5974
f. 720.304.3637

Mailing Address:
Simple Moves
7746 Fairview Road
Boulder, CO 80303

Made in the USA
Monee, IL
11 January 2021